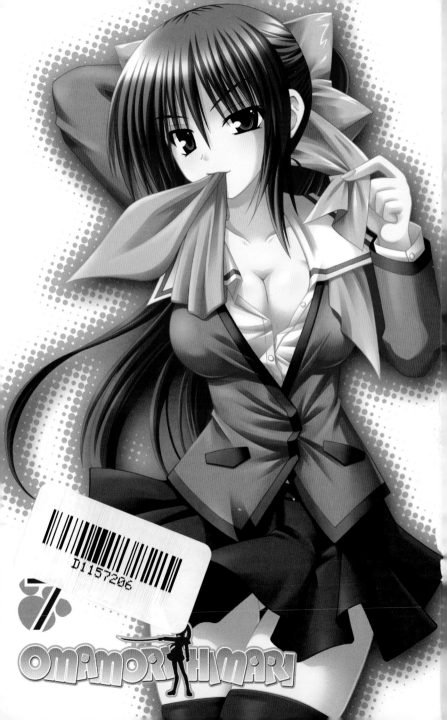

OMAMORI HIMARI

CONTENTS

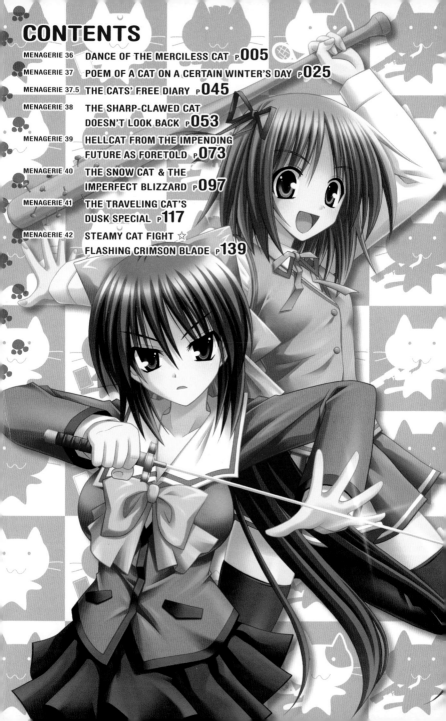

MENAGERIE 36 DANCE OF THE MERCILESS CAT p005

MENAGERIE 37 POEM OF A CAT ON A CERTAIN WINTER'S DAY p025

MENAGERIE 37.5 THE CATS' FREE DIARY p045

MENAGERIE 38 THE SHARP-CLAWED CAT
DOESN'T LOOK BACK p053

MENAGERIE 39 HELLCAT FROM THE IMPENDING
FUTURE AS FORETOLD p073

MENAGERIE 40 THE SNOW CAT & THE
IMPERFECT BLIZZARD p097

MENAGERIE 41 THE TRAVELING CAT'S
DUSK SPECIAL p117

MENAGERIE 42 STEAMY CAT FIGHT ☆
FLASHING CRIMSON BLADE p139

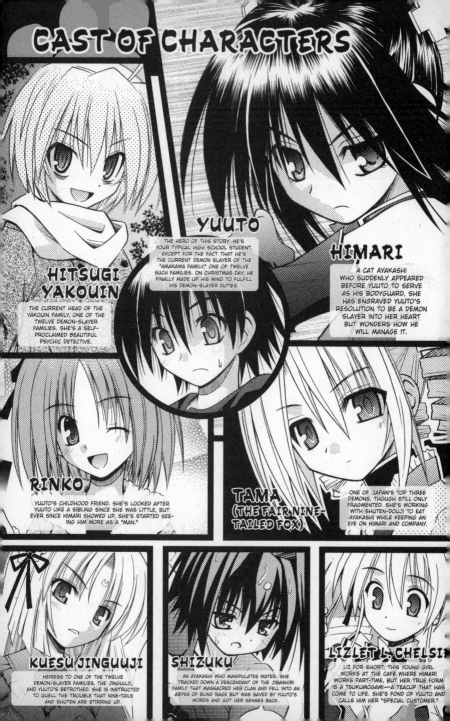

CAST OF CHARACTERS

YUUTO

THE HERO OF THIS STORY. HE'S YOUR TYPICAL HIGH SCHOOL STUDENT, EXCEPT FOR THE FACT THAT HE'S THE CURRENT DEMON SLAYER OF THE "AMAKAWA FAMILY," ONE OF TWELVE SUCH FAMILIES. ON CHRISTMAS DAY, HE FINALLY MADE UP HIS MIND TO FULFILL HIS DEMON-SLAYER DUTIES.

HITSUGI YAKOUIN

THE CURRENT HEAD OF THE YAKOUIN FAMILY, ONE OF THE TWELVE DEMON-SLAYER FAMILIES. SHE'S A SELF-PROCLAIMED BEAUTIFUL PSYCHIC DETECTIVE.

HIMARI

A CAT AYAKASHI WHO SUDDENLY APPEARED BEFORE YUUTO TO SERVE AS HIS BODYGUARD. SHE HAS ENGRAVED YUUTO'S RESOLUTION TO BE A DEMON SLAYER INTO HER HEART BUT WONDERS HOW HE WILL MANAGE IT.

RINKO

YUUTO'S CHILDHOOD FRIEND. SHE'S LOOKED AFTER YUUTO LIKE A SIBLING SINCE SHE WAS LITTLE, BUT EVER SINCE HIMARI SHOWED UP, SHE'S STARTED SEEING HIM MORE AS A "MAN."

TAMA (THE FAIR NINE-TAILED FOX)

ONE OF JAPAN'S TOP THREE DEMONS, THOUGH STILL ONLY FRAGMENTED. SHE'S WORKING WITH SHUTEN-DOUJI TO EAT AYAKASHI WHILE KEEPING AN EYE ON HIMARI AND COMPANY.

KUESU JINGUUJI

HEIRESS TO ONE OF THE TWELVE DEMON-SLAYER FAMILIES, THE JINGUUJI, AND YUUTO'S BETROTHED. SHE IS INSTRUCTED TO QUELL THE TROUBLE THAT NINE-TAILS AND SHUTEN ARE STIRRING UP.

SHIZUKU

AN AYAKASHI WHO MANIPULATES WATER. SHE TRACKED DOWN A DESCENDANT OF THE JIBASHIRI FAMILY THAT MASSACRED HER CLAN AND FELL INTO AN ABYSS OF BLIND RAGE BUT WAS SAVED BY YUUTO'S WORDS AND GOT HER SENSES BACK.

LIZLET L. CHELSI

LIZ FOR SHORT, THIS YOUNG GIRL WORKS AT THE CAFÉ WHERE HIMARI WORKS PART-TIME, BUT HER TRUE FORM IS A TSUKUMOGAMI—A TEACUP THAT HAS COME TO LIFE. SHE'S FOND OF YUUTO AND CALLS HIM HER "SPECIAL CUSTOMER."

❖THE❖STORY❖SO❖FAR❖

YUUTO AMAKAWA IS A HIGH SCHOOLER WITH A SEVERE ALLERGY TO CATS.
WHO SHOULD APPEAR BEFORE HIM ONE DAY OTHER THAN A FELINE AYAKASHI, HIMARI?

"I WILL PROTECT YOU, YOUNG LORD."

SUCH IS THE PROCLAMATION MADE BY HIMARI, HAVING BEEN GIVEN THE DUTY OF PROTECTING YUUTO,
THANKS TO A PLEDGE MADE LONG AGO. BUT YUUTO ALSO HAS TO DEAL WITH HIS NEIGHBOR AND CHILD-
HOOD FRIEND, RINKO, AS WELL AS THE AYAKASHI SHIZUKU, WHO WAS SWAYED BY YUUTO'S KINDNESS
AND DECIDED TO LIVE WITH HIM. WITH ALL THESE GIRLS IN HIS LIFE, YUUTO'S DAYS QUICKLY BECOME
OFF-THE-WALL AND FULL OF FUN WITH NO END OF SURPRISES.

WELL, THESE DAYS WERE SUPPOSED TO BE FUN-FILLED AND RELAXED. BUT DEEP WITHIN SHIZUKU, A
FLAME OF REVENGE STILL SMOLDERS. THAT'S WHEN SHE COMES UPON A MEMBER OF THE JIBASHIRI,
THE DEMON-SLAYER FAMILY WHO WIPED OUT HER KIND LONG AGO. THANKS TO THE MACHINATIONS OF
KUESU, RANKA MIKARI, A JIBASHIRI DESCENDANT, IS PITTED AGAINST SHIZUKU, WHO GLADLY TAKES THIS
OPPORTUNITY TO AVENGE HER FAMILY.

"WATER IS SO VERSATILE...
I CAN CRUSH YOU, DROWN YOU, OR DISMEMBER YOU...
WHICH SHOULD I GO WITH...YOU KNOW?"

FROM WITHIN SHIZUKU'S HEART, YUUTO'S VOICE OF REASON RINGS LOUD AND CLEAR, STATING THAT HER
BEING AN AYAKASHI DOESN'T MEAN SHE HAS TO FIGHT AND EVERYONE SHOULD JUST GET ALONG. BUT IN
THE FACE OF HER RAGING HATRED, HIS WORDS FAIL TO SINK IN, AND SHIZUKU MOVES IN FOR THE KILL.

HAVING CAST ASIDE A CHANCE AT A NEW LIFE WITH YUUTO AND ALL HER FRIENDS, SHIZUKU CHOOSES
INSTEAD TO THROW HER VERY BODY AND SOUL INTO AN ABYSS OF HATE. THUS, KUESU DECIDES TO PASS
JUDGMENT ON HER AS A DEMON SLAYER.

"YOU ALONE SURVIVED, AND THE JIBASHIRI PERISHED.
YOU WERE BLESSED WITH DECADES MORE LIFE THAN THEY,
DON'T YOU SEE?"

AT THAT MOMENT, A BLADE SUDDENLY SWINGS DOWN. HIMARI APPEARS WITH HER
SWORD IN HAND AND YUUTO IN TOW TO SAVE SHIZUKU. AS YUUTO SHOWS SIGNS
OF UNLEASHING HIS LIGHT FERRY, SHIZUKU GRITS HER TEETH AND CHARGES
IN FOR THE ATTACK. BUT INSTEAD OF LEVELING HIS POWER AT HER, YUUTO
DRAWS HER INTO HIS ARMS.

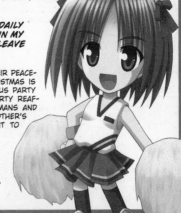

"IF YOU FORCED YOUR WAY INTO MY DAILY
LIFE AND MADE YOURSELF AT HOME IN MY
HOME, THEN YOU'RE FORBIDDEN TO LEAVE
WITHOUT PERMISSION!"

SHIZUKU BREAKS DOWN IN TEARS, AND THEREAFTER THEIR PEACE-
FUL DAYS GRADUALLY RETURN TO NORMAL. SOON, CHRISTMAS IS
UPON THEM. HIMARI AND THE GANG ENJOY A BOISTEROUS PARTY
WITH KUESU AND RINKO. SEEING EVERYONE AT THE PARTY REAF-
FIRMS IN YUUTO'S MIND THAT IT IS POSSIBLE FOR HUMANS AND
AYAKASHI TO OCCUPY THE SAME SPACE AND ENJOY EACH OTHER'S
COMPANY. HE CONFIDES TO HIMARI THAT HE WILL FIGHT TO
PROTECT THAT HARMONY IF HE MUST.

"FROM TODAY FORWARD, YOU ARE A
TRUE DEMON SLAYER."

HIMARI ENGRAVES YUUTO'S RESOLUTION INTO HER HEART.
SUDDENLY, AN AYAKASHI SENT BY THE NINE-TAILS
APPEARS. BUT WHY!?

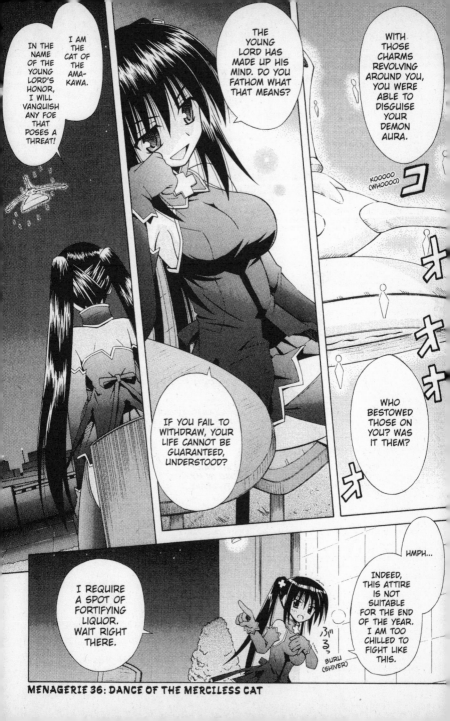

MENAGERIE 36: DANCE OF THE MERCILESS CAT

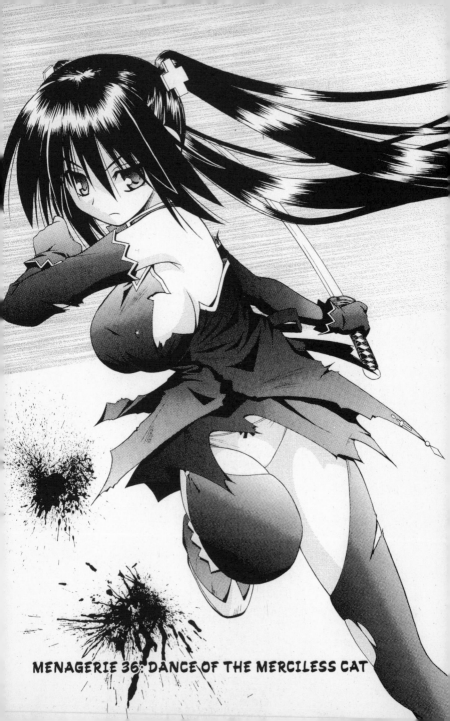

MENAGERIE 36: DANCE OF THE MERCILESS CAT

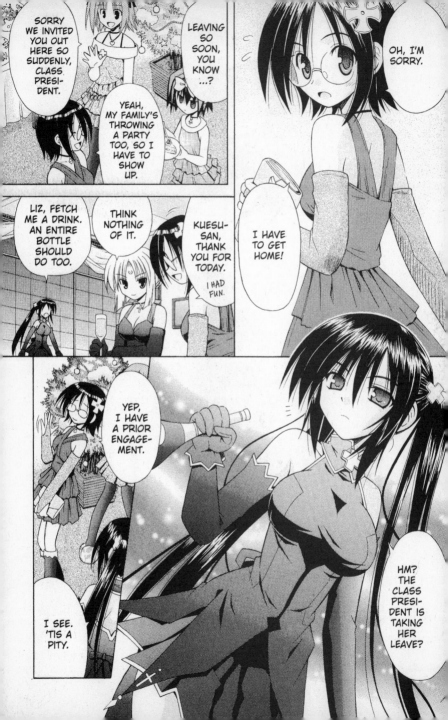

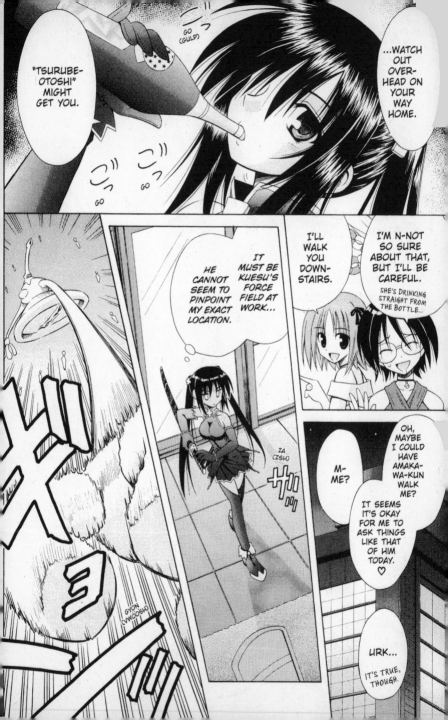

"TSURUBE-OTOSHI" MIGHT GET YOU.

...WATCH OUT OVERHEAD ON YOUR WAY HOME.

GO (GULP)

GO

GO

GO

HE CANNOT SEEM TO PINPOINT MY EXACT LOCATION.

IT MUST BE KUESU'S FORCE FIELD AT WORK...

I'LL WALK YOU DOWNSTAIRS.

I'M N-NOT SO SURE ABOUT THAT, BUT I'LL BE CAREFUL.

SHE'S DRINKING STRAIGHT FROM THE BOTTLE...

ZA (ZSH)

OH, MAYBE I COULD HAVE AMAKAWA-KUN WALK ME?

IT SEEMS IT'S OKAY FOR ME TO ASK THINGS LIKE THAT OF HIM TODAY. ♡

M-ME?

URK...

IT'S TRUE, THOUGH.

GYON (WOOSH)

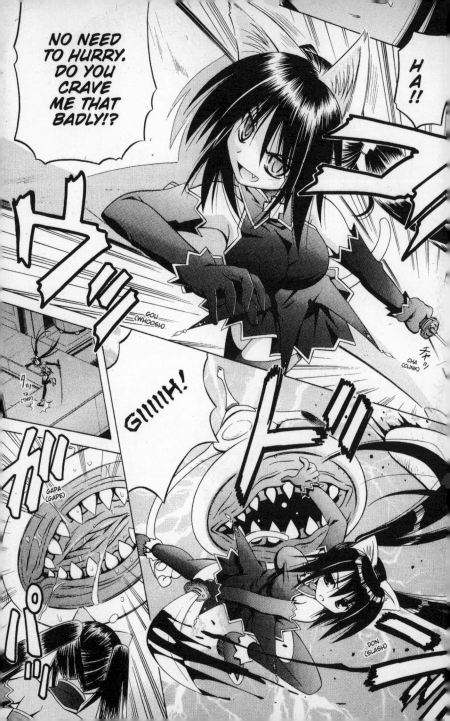

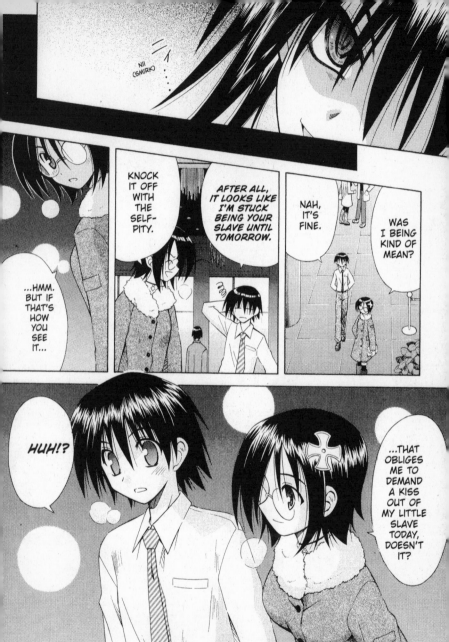

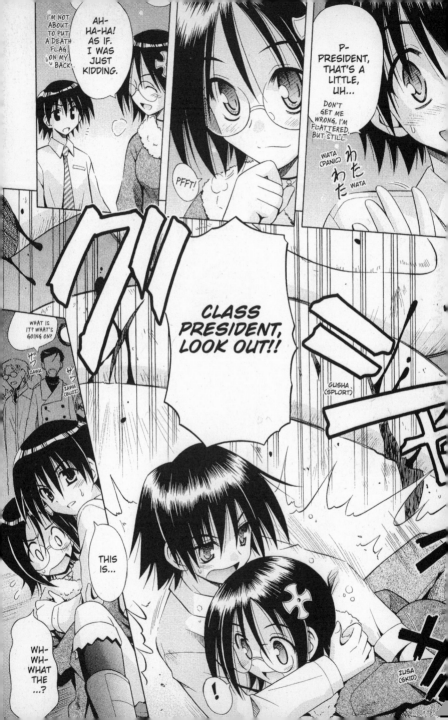

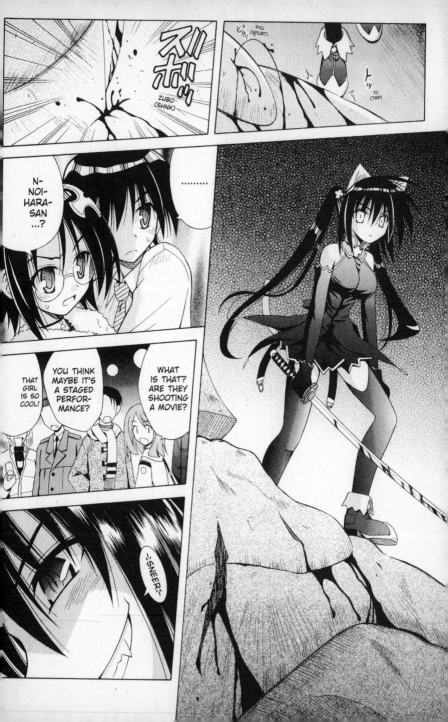

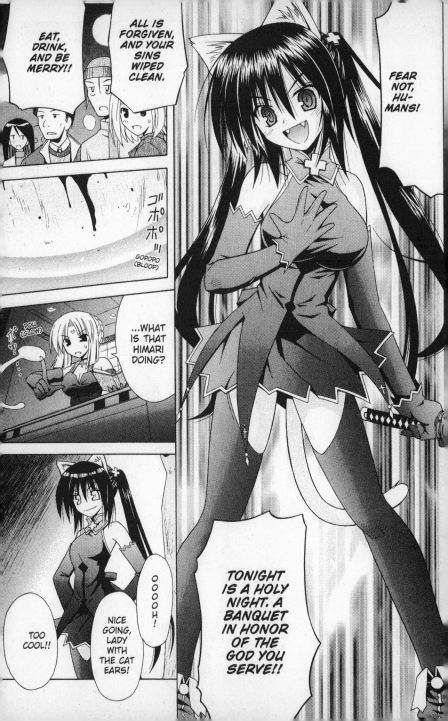

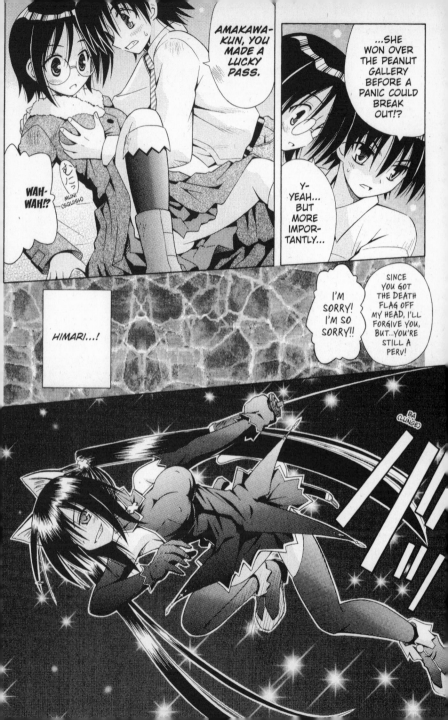

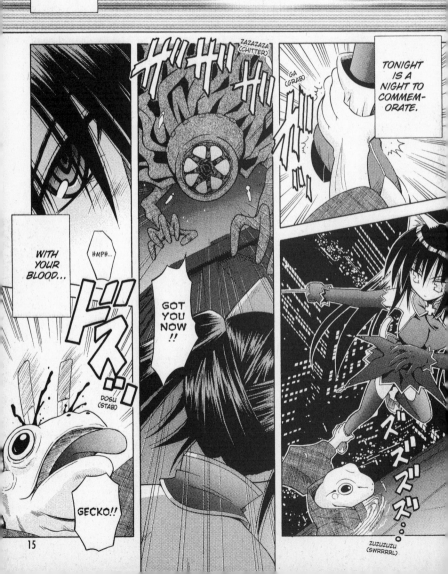

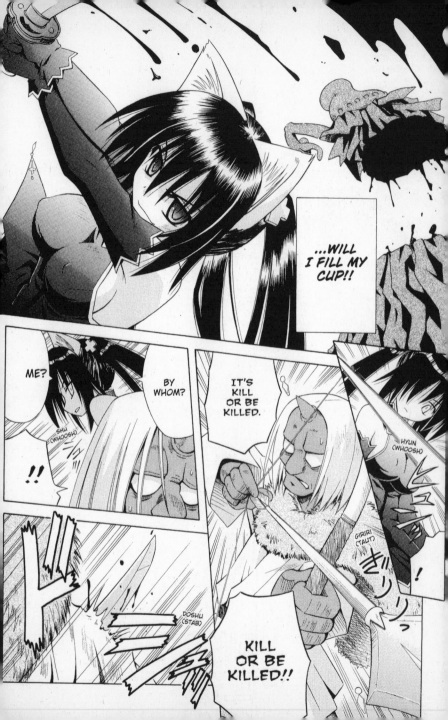

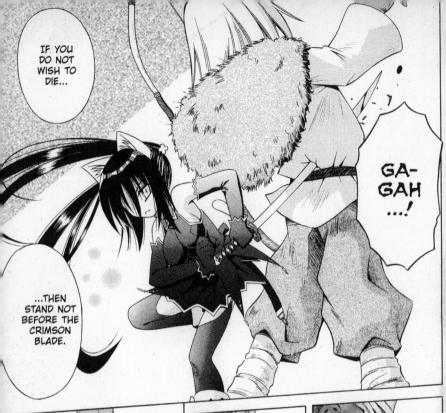

IF YOU DO NOT WISH TO DIE...

GA-GAH....!

...THEN STAND NOT BEFORE THE CRIMSON BLADE.

BECOME A LUMP OF FLESH.

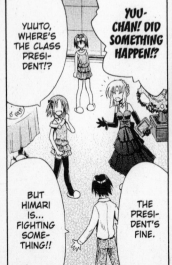

YUUTO, WHERE'S THE CLASS PRESIDENT!?

YUU-CHAN! DID SOMETHING HAPPEN!?

BUT HIMARI IS... FIGHTING SOMETHING!!

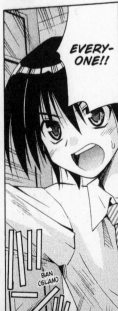

EVERYONE!!

THE PRESIDENT'S FINE.

BAN (SLAM)

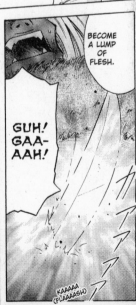

GUH! GAA-AAH!

KAAAAA (FLAAAASH)

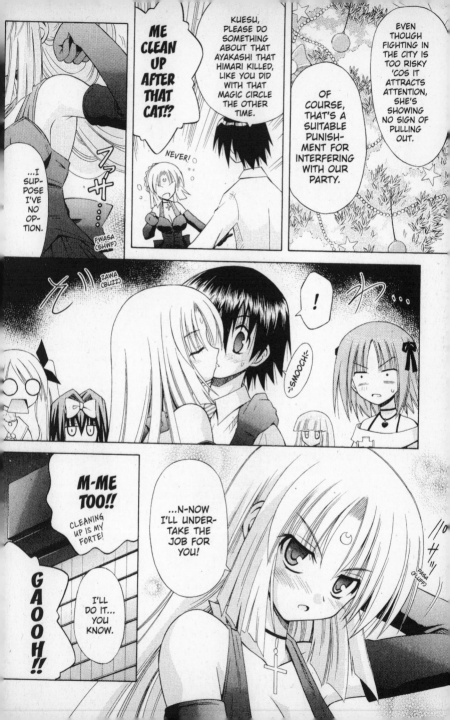

ME CLEAN UP AFTER THAT CAT!?

KUESU, PLEASE DO SOMETHING ABOUT THAT AYAKASHI THAT HIMARI KILLED, LIKE YOU DID WITH THAT MAGIC CIRCLE THE OTHER TIME.

OF COURSE, THAT'S A SUITABLE PUNISHMENT FOR INTERFERING WITH OUR PARTY.

EVEN THOUGH FIGHTING IN THE CITY IS TOO RISKY 'COS IT ATTRACTS ATTENTION, SHE'S SHOWING NO SIGN OF PULLING OUT.

NEVER!

...I SUPPOSE I'VE NO OPTION.

FWASA (SHWF)

ZUZU

ZAWA (BUZZ)

-:SMOOCH:-

-:SMOOCH:-

!

M-ME TOO!!

CLEANING UP IS MY FORTE!

...N-NOW I'LL UNDERTAKE THE JOB FOR YOU!

GAOOH!!

I'LL DO IT... YOU KNOW.

PASA (SLIP?)

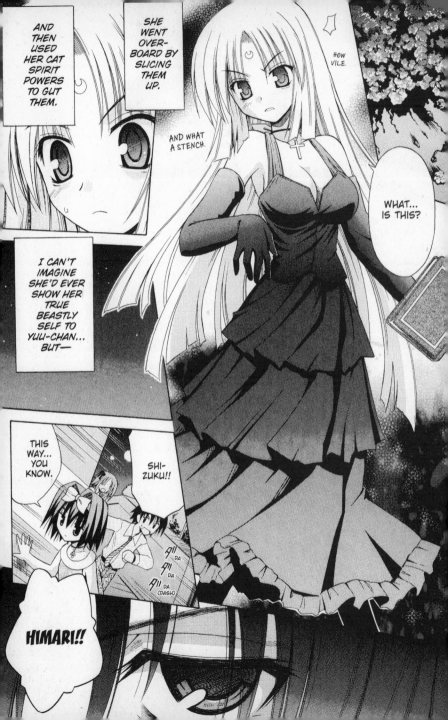

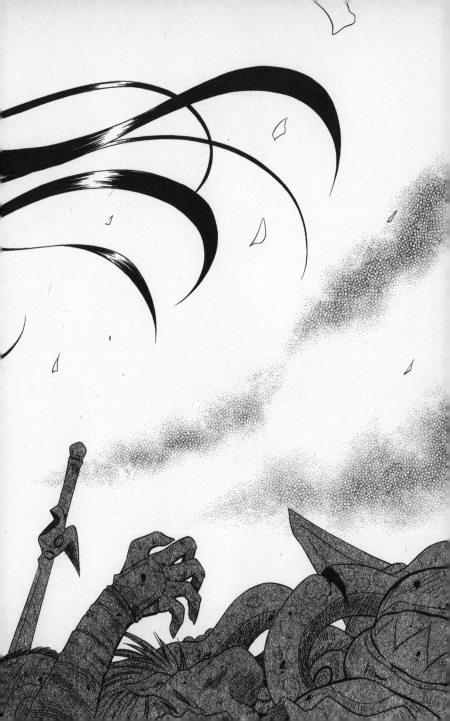

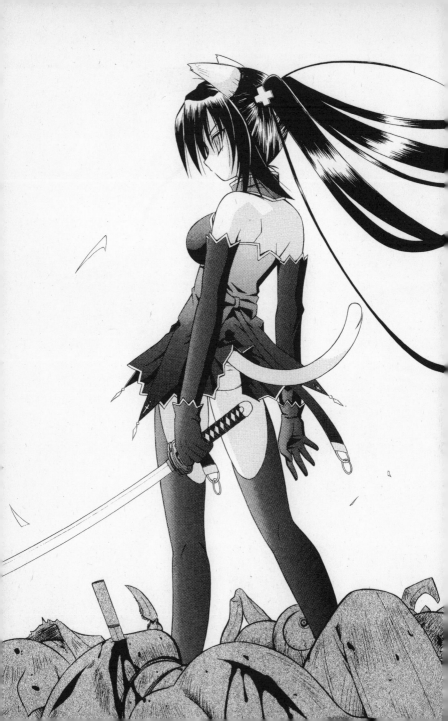

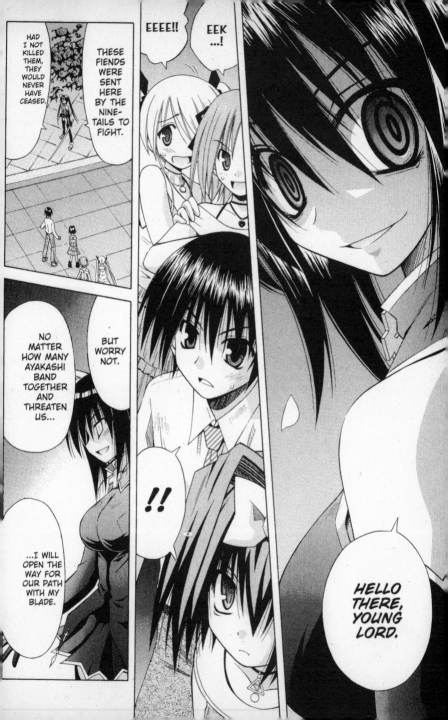

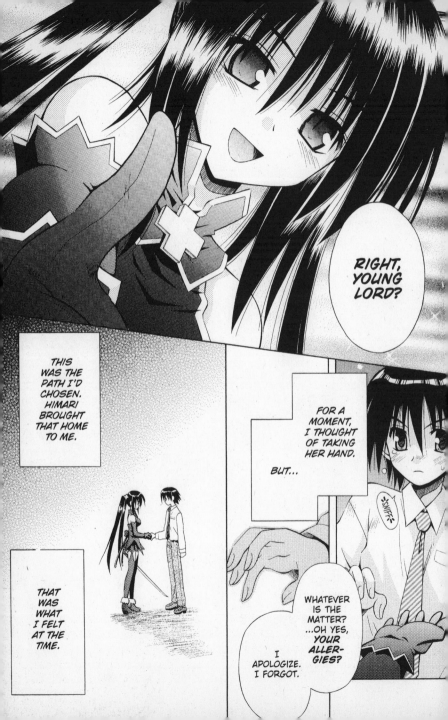

RIGHT, YOUNG LORD?

THIS WAS THE PATH I'D CHOSEN. HIMARI BROUGHT THAT HOME TO ME.

FOR A MOMENT, I THOUGHT OF TAKING HER HAND.

BUT...

THAT WAS WHAT I FELT AT THE TIME.

≈SNIFF≈

WHATEVER IS THE MATTER? ...OH YES, YOUR ALLERGIES?

I APOLOGIZE. I FORGOT.

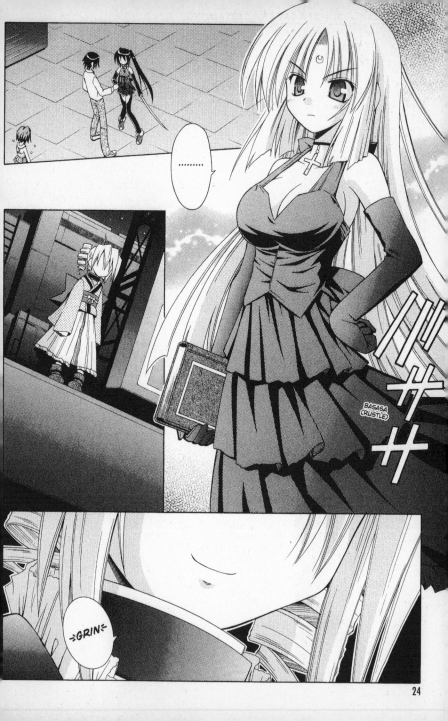

....

BASASA
(RUSTLE)

≥GRIN≤

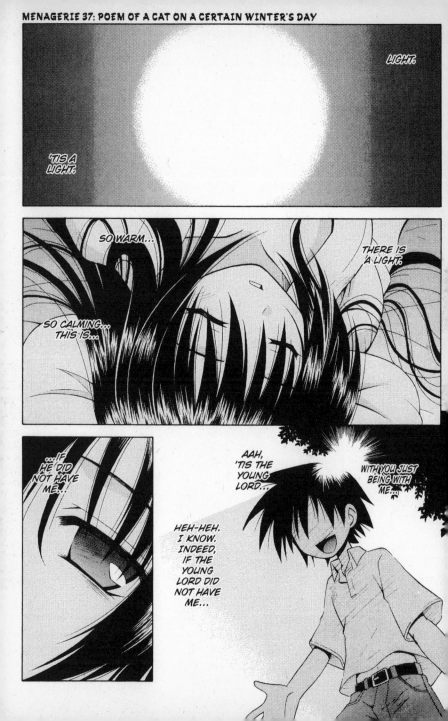

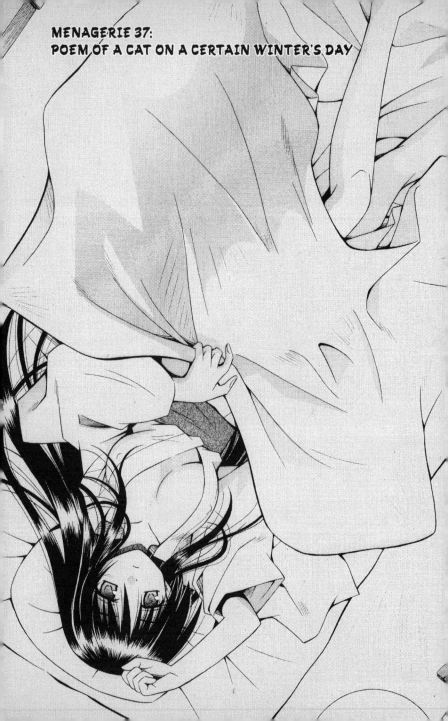

MENAGERIE 37:
POEM OF A CAT ON A CERTAIN WINTER'S DAY

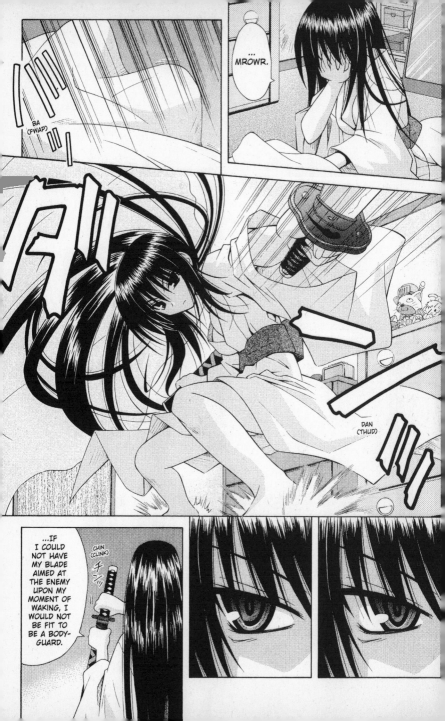

...
MROWR.

BA
(FWAP)

DAN
(THUD)

...IF I COULD NOT HAVE MY BLADE AIMED AT THE ENEMY UPON MY MOMENT OF WAKING, I WOULD NOT BE FIT TO BE A BODY-GUARD.

CHIN
(CLINK)

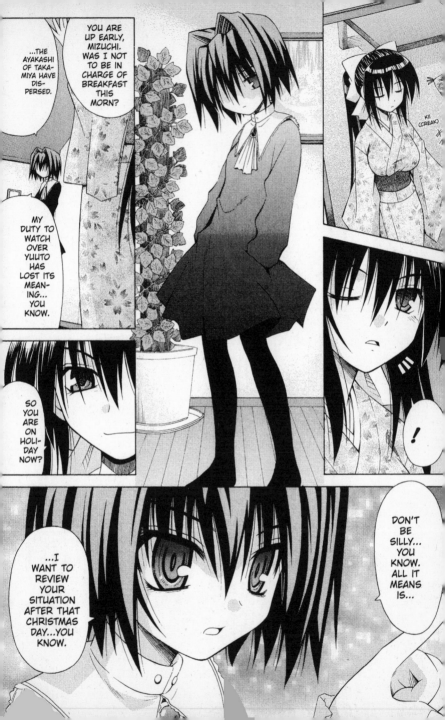

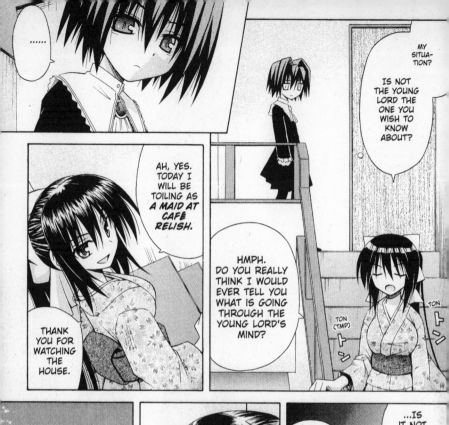

......

MY SITUATION?

IS NOT THE YOUNG LORD THE ONE YOU WISH TO KNOW ABOUT?

AH, YES. TODAY I WILL BE TOILING AS *A MAID AT CAFÉ RELISH.*

THANK YOU FOR WATCHING THE HOUSE.

HMPH. DO YOU REALLY THINK I WOULD EVER TELL YOU WHAT IS GOING THROUGH THE YOUNG LORD'S MIND?

TON (TMP)

TON

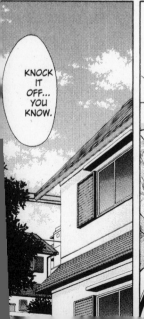

KNOCK IT OFF... YOU KNOW.

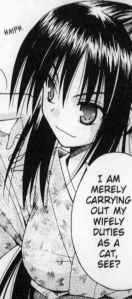

HMPH.

LATELY YOUR MISO SOUP HAS *TAKEN ON THAT FLAVOR TOO...* YOU KNOW.

I AM MERELY CARRYING OUT MY WIFELY DUTIES AS A CAT, SEE?

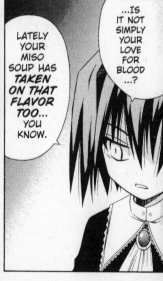

...IS IT NOT SIMPLY YOUR LOVE FOR BLOOD...?

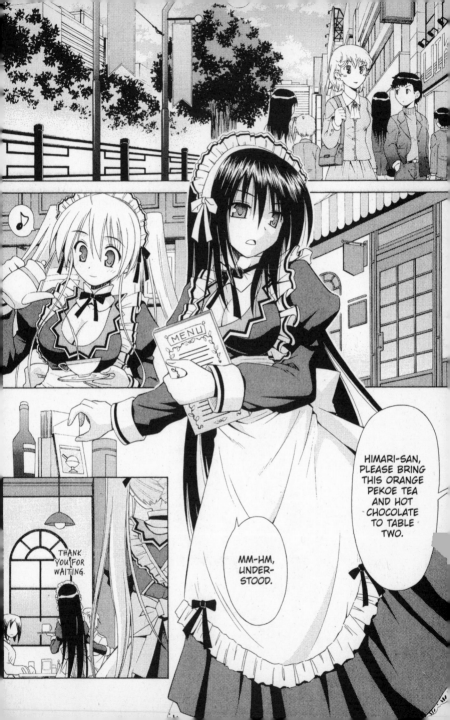

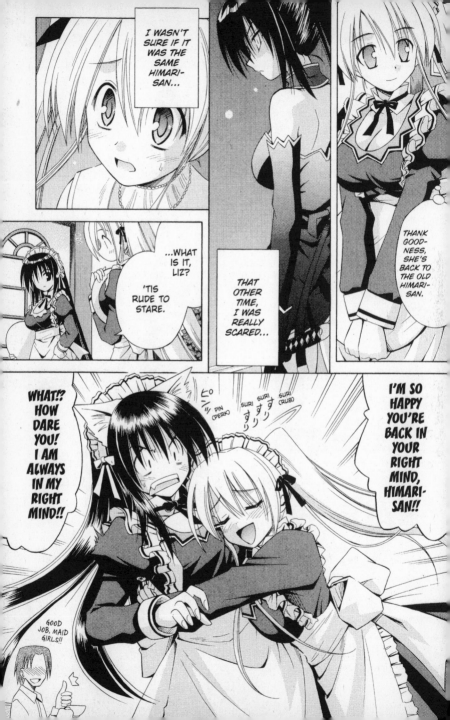

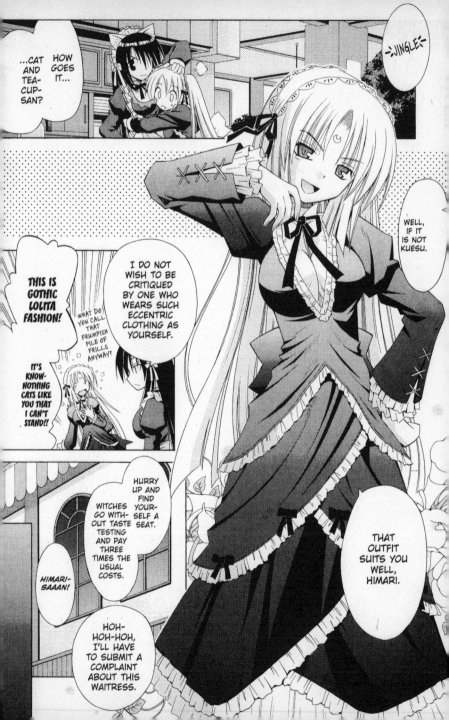

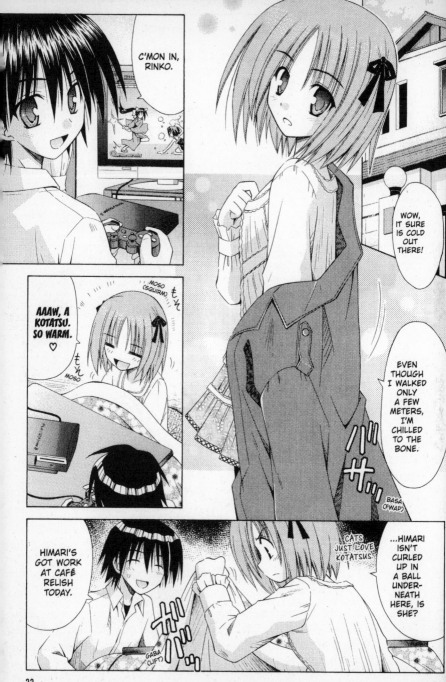

C'MON IN, RINKO.

WOW, IT SURE IS COLD OUT THERE!

EVEN THOUGH I WALKED ONLY A FEW METERS, I'M CHILLED TO THE BONE.

BASA (FWAP)

MOSO (SQUIRM)

AAAW, A KOTATSU. SO WARM. ♡

MOSO

HIMARI'S GOT WORK AT CAFÉ RELISH TODAY.

CATS JUST LOVE KOTATSUS.

...HIMARI ISN'T CURLED UP IN A BALL UNDERNEATH HERE, IS SHE?

GABA (LIFT)

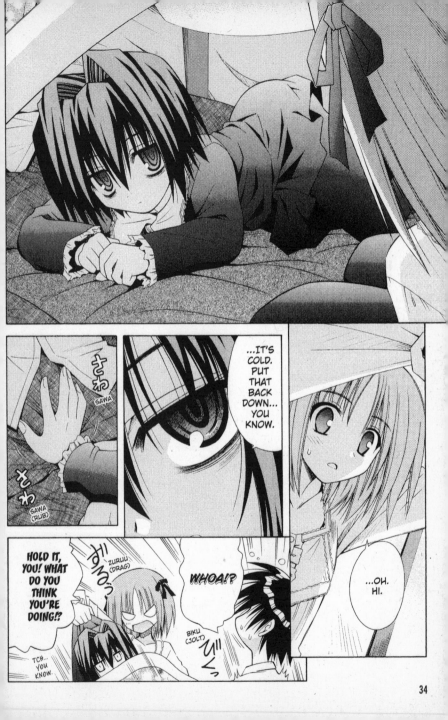

...IT'S COLD. PUT THAT BACK DOWN... YOU KNOW.

SAWA

SAWA (RUB)

...OH. HI.

HOLD IT, YOU! WHAT DO YOU THINK YOU'RE DOING!?

ZURUU (DRAG)

WHOA!?

BIKU (JOLT)

TCH... YOU KNOW.

34

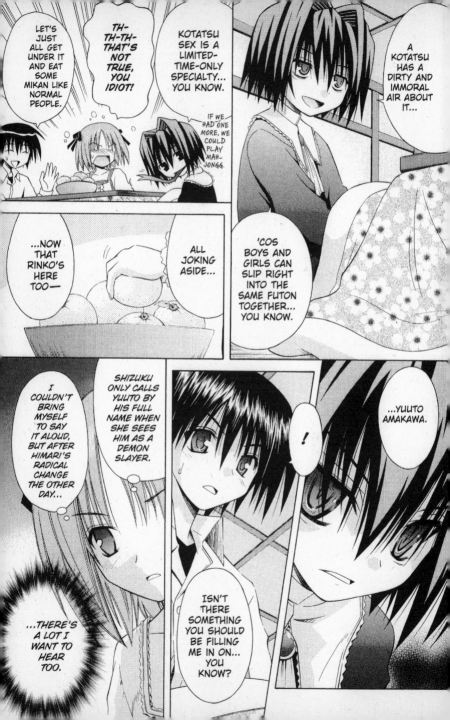

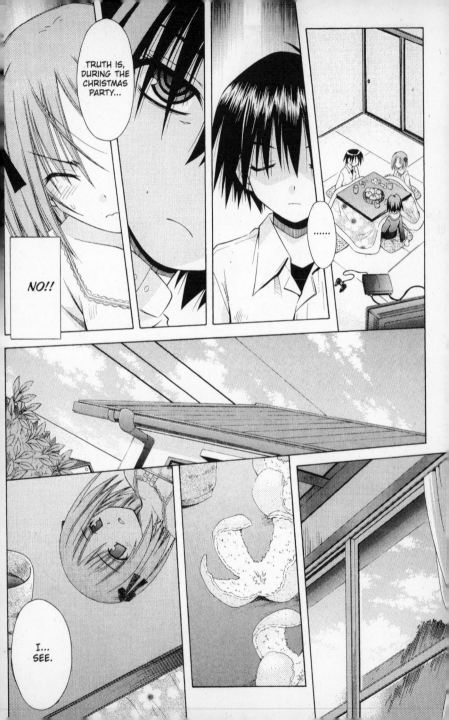

...HAVE DECIDED TO FIGHT AS YUUTO AMAKAWA, THE DEMON SLAYER...YOU KNOW.

SO YOU...

HA HA, I GUESS SO.

...PLAYED A PART IN MAKING YOU DECIDE THIS. HOW IRONIC.

...I CAN'T BELIEVE MY VENGEFUL HEART...

HAAH...

CHRISTMAS NIGHT, I THOUGHT SOMETHING WAS UP WHEN I SAW HIMARI.

...I SEE. SO YOU'VE MADE UP YOUR MIND.

YUUTO'S A DEMON SLAYER, HIMARI AND THE OTHERS ARE AYAKASHI, AND I'M JUST A REGULAR HUMAN...

DEEP DOWN IN MY HEART, I KNEW WE LIVED IN DIFFERENT WORLDS.

I ALWAYS SORT OF KNEW ALL THIS TIME.

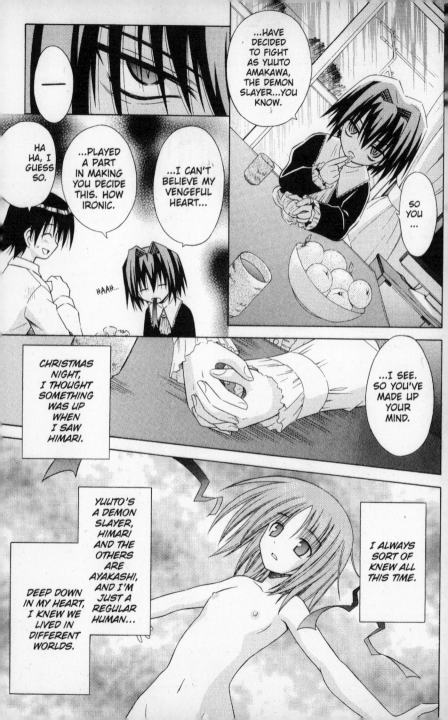

...DON'T APOLO-GIZE.

I'M SORRY, RINKO.

JUST LIKE HOW THEY SUDDENLY SHOWED UP ONE DAY...

...I'M AFRAID HE'S GONNA GO OFF SOMEWHERE FAR AWAY ALL OF A SUDDEN AND LEAVE ME BEHIND...

...I NEVER DID A THING FOR HIM.

EVEN THOUGH I HAD THAT VAGUE PRE-MONITION, I CLUNG TIGHTLY TO MY DAILY LIFE, BELIEVING IT WOULD NEVER CHANGE.

EVEN THOUGH IT WAS SO OBVIOUS THAT AFTER LEARNING HIS FAMILY'S SECRET, YUUTO'S BEEN TORN APART INSIDE, I...

I CAN BARELY CALL MYSELF HIS CHILDHOOD FRIEND LIKE THIS...

...REALLY, RINKO. I'M SORRY TO ASK SOMETHING SO SELFISH, BUT...

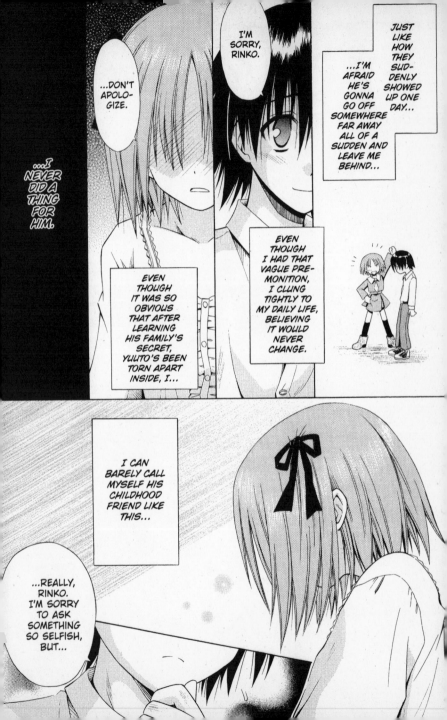

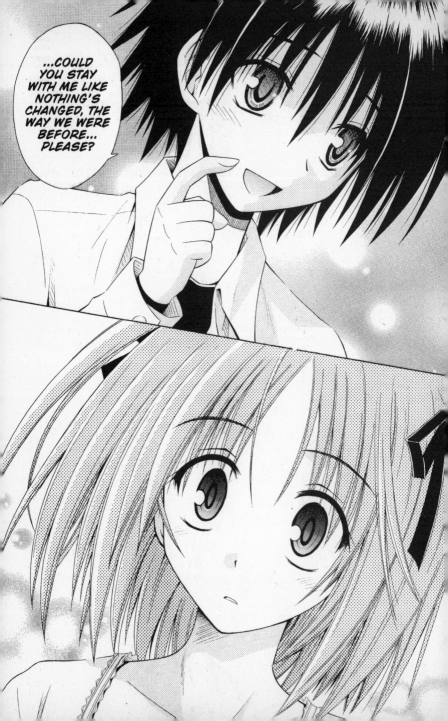

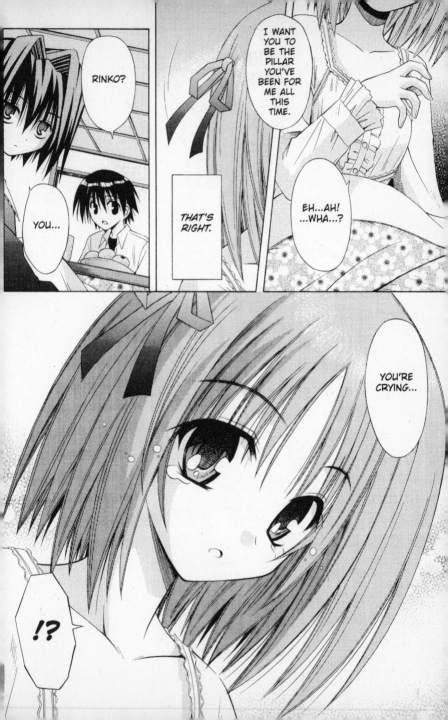

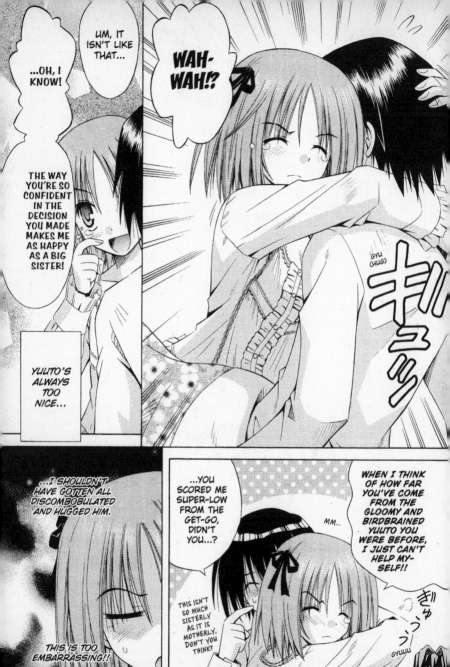

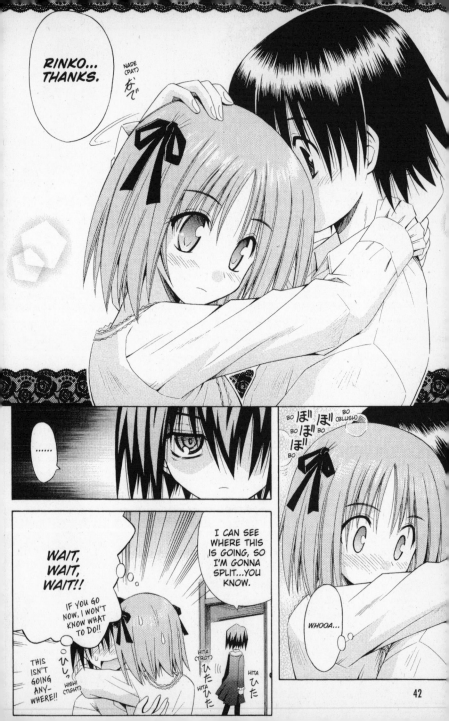

RINKO... THANKS.

NADE (PAT)
なで

......

BO (BLUSH)
ぼ ぼ ぼ
ぼ ぼ BO
BO BO

WHOOA...

WAIT, WAIT, WAIT!!

IF YOU GO NOW, I WON'T KNOW WHAT TO DO!!

THIS ISN'T GOING ANY- WHERE!!

HISH! (TIGHT)

I CAN SEE WHERE THIS IS GOING, SO I'M GONNA SPLIT...YOU KNOW.

HITA (TROT)
ひたひた
ひた
HITA

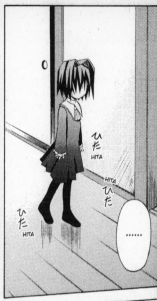

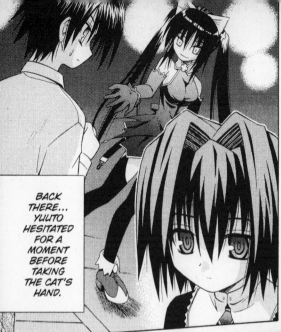

ひた
HITA

ひた
HITA

ひた
HITA

ひた
HITA

......

BACK THERE... YUUTO HESITATED FOR A MOMENT BEFORE TAKING THE CAT'S HAND.

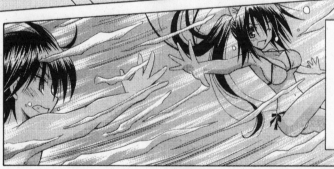

WHEREAS THE FIRST TIME THEY FOUGHT, THE TWO CLASPED HANDS WITHOUT A SECOND THOUGHT...

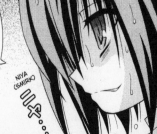

...THERE'S STILL A CHANCE... YOU KNOW.

NIYA (SMIRK)

KOTATSU SEX, KOTATSU SEX, KOTATSU SEX...

WH- WHAT AM I SUPPOSED TO DO...?

BO
BO
BO

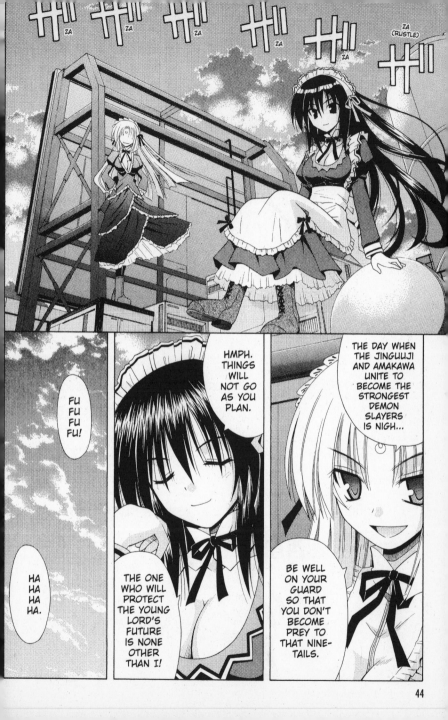

ZA

ZA

ZA

ZA

ZA
(RUSTLE)

FU
FU
FU
FU!

HA
HA
HA
HA.

HMPH. THINGS WILL NOT GO AS YOU PLAN.

THE ONE WHO WILL PROTECT THE YOUNG LORD'S FUTURE IS NONE OTHER THAN I!

THE DAY WHEN THE JINGUUJI AND AMAKAWA UNITE TO BECOME THE STRONGEST DEMON SLAYERS IS NIGH...

BE WELL ON YOUR GUARD SO THAT YOU DON'T BECOME PREY TO THAT NINE-TAILS.

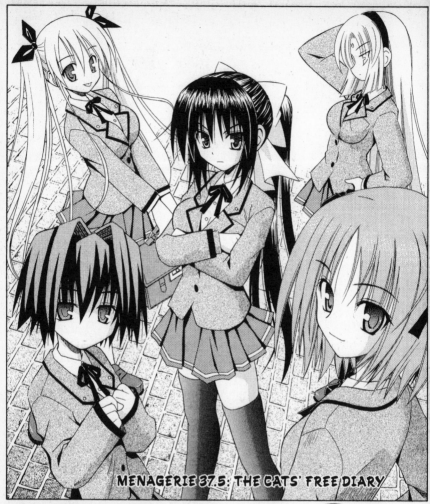

MENAGERIE 37.5: THE CATS' FREE DIARY

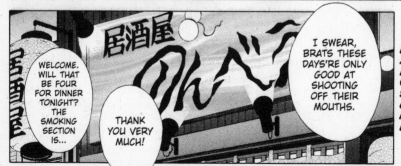

WELCOME. WILL THAT BE FOUR FOR DINNER TONIGHT? THE SMOKING SECTION IS...

THANK YOU VERY MUCH!

I SWEAR, BRATS THESE DAYS'RE ONLY GOOD AT SHOOTING OFF THEIR MOUTHS.

EXPOSURE

SIGN: BAR NONBOU

THEY JUST DON'T LISTEN!

AND THEY NEVER TAKE THEIR TEACHERS SERIOUSLY!

NIKO (BEAM)

NIKO

OH, SAE-CHAN. YOU'RE JUST SO AMUSING, EVEN WHEN YOU'RE BITCHING ABOUT THINGS.

WHAT'S SO FUNNY, YUUKO?

DAN (SLAM)

SIGN: DRAFT BEER YUUHI

COMPARED TO THE PERSONAL STRIFE I'M GOING THROUGH, THIS DOESN'T EVEN MERIT BITCHING.

GUBII! (CHUG)

MMM...

YOU TRY TAKING ON AN EXTRA CLASS. THEN YOU'LL KNOW WHAT HARD WORK IS.

HA! SPARE ME.

I COULD NEVER. I JUST DON'T HAVE THE PRESENCE FOR IT.

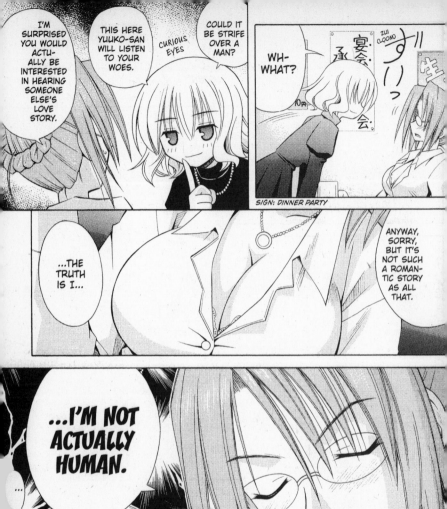

I'M SURPRISED YOU WOULD ACTUALLY BE INTERESTED IN HEARING SOMEONE ELSE'S LOVE STORY.

THIS HERE YUUKO-SAN WILL LISTEN TO YOUR WOES.

CURIOUS EYES

COULD IT BE STRIFE OVER A MAN?

WH-WHAT?

ZUI CLOONO

SIGN: DINNER PARTY

...THE TRUTH IS I...

ANYWAY, SORRY, BUT IT'S NOT SUCH A ROMANTIC STORY AS ALL THAT.

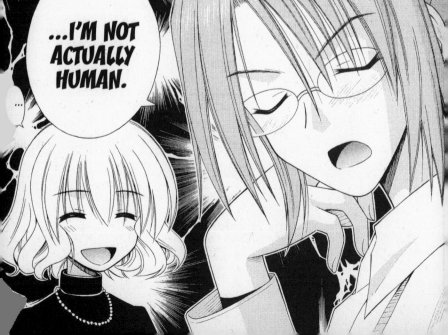

...I'M NOT ACTUALLY HUMAN.

...

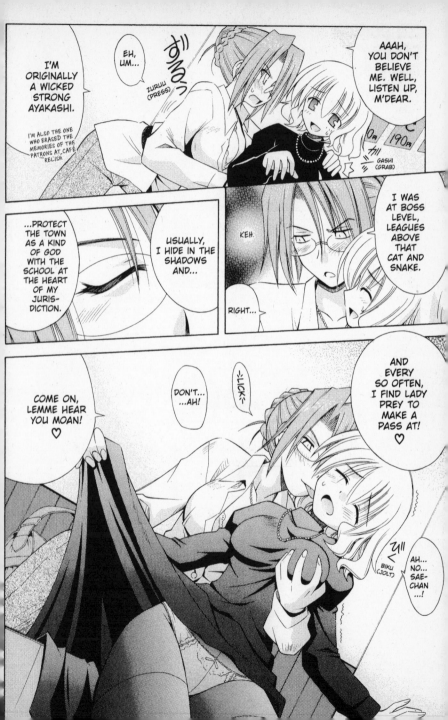

I'M ORIGINALLY A WICKED STRONG AYAKASHI.

I'M ALSO THE ONE WHO ERASED THE MEMORIES OF THE PATRONS AT CAFÉ RELISH.

EH, UM...

ZURUU (PRESS)

AAAH, YOU DON'T BELIEVE ME. WELL, LISTEN UP, M'DEAR.

GASHI (GRAB)

...PROTECT THE TOWN AS A KIND OF GOD WITH THE SCHOOL AT THE HEART OF MY JURIS-DICTION.

USUALLY, I HIDE IN THE SHADOWS AND...

KEH.

RIGHT...

I WAS AT BOSS LEVEL, LEAGUES ABOVE THAT CAT AND SNAKE.

COME ON, LEMME HEAR YOU MOAN! ♥

DON'T... ...AH!

LICK

AND EVERY SO OFTEN, I FIND LADY PREY TO MAKE A PASS AT! ♥

BIKU (JOLT)

AH... NO... SAE-CHAN ...!

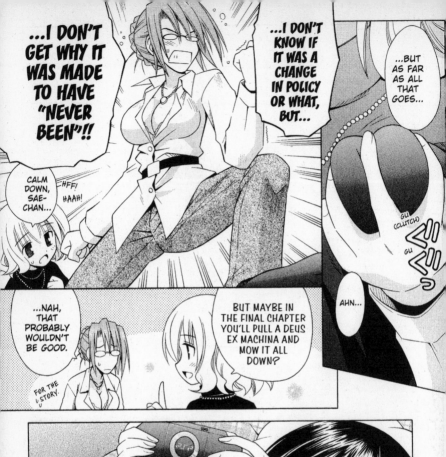

...I DON'T GET WHY IT WAS MADE TO HAVE "NEVER BEEN"!!

CALM DOWN, SAE-CHAN...

HFF! HAAH!

...I DON'T KNOW IF IT WAS A CHANGE IN POLICY OR WHAT, BUT...

...BUT AS FAR AS ALL THAT GOES...

GU (CCLUTCH)

GU

AHN...

...NAH, THAT PROBABLY WOULDN'T BE GOOD.

FOR THE STORY.

BUT MAYBE IN THE FINAL CHAPTER YOU'LL PULL A DEUS EX MACHINA AND MOW IT ALL DOWN?

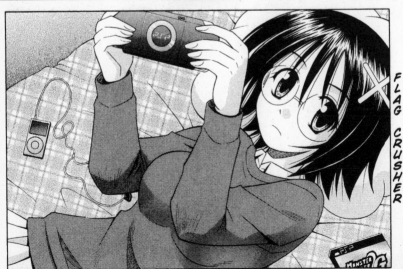

FLAG CRUSHER

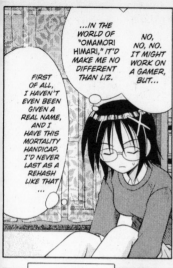

...IN THE WORLD OF "OMAMORI HIMARI," IT'D MAKE ME NO DIFFERENT THAN LIZ.

NO, NO, NO. IT MIGHT WORK ON A GAMER, BUT...

FIRST OF ALL, I HAVEN'T EVEN BEEN GIVEN A REAL NAME, AND I HAVE THIS MORTALITY HANDICAP. I'D NEVER LAST AS A REHASH LIKE THAT...

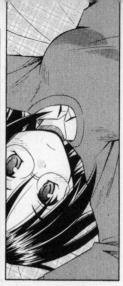

"CLASS PRESIDENT GETS CAUGHT UP IN BATTLE AND DIES."

I AVOIDED A DEATH FLAG LIKE THAT.

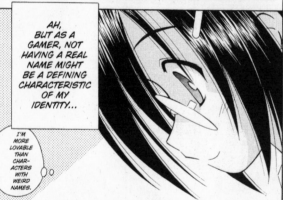

AH, BUT AS A GAMER, NOT HAVING A REAL NAME MIGHT BE A DEFINING CHARACTERISTIC OF MY IDENTITY...

I'M MORE LOVABLE THAN CHARACTERS WITH WEIRD NAMES.

BUT WHAT ABOUT THIS LOVE FLAG FOR AMAKAWA-KUN WHO JUST SAVED ME...?

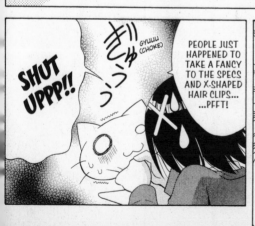

GYUUU (CHOKE)

SHUT UPPP!!

PEOPLE JUST HAPPENED TO TAKE A FANCY TO THE SPECS AND X-SHAPED HAIR CLIPS... ...PFFT!

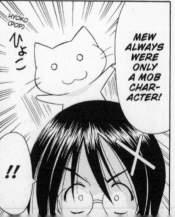

HYOKO (POP)

MEW ALWAYS WERE ONLY A MOB CHARACTER!

!!

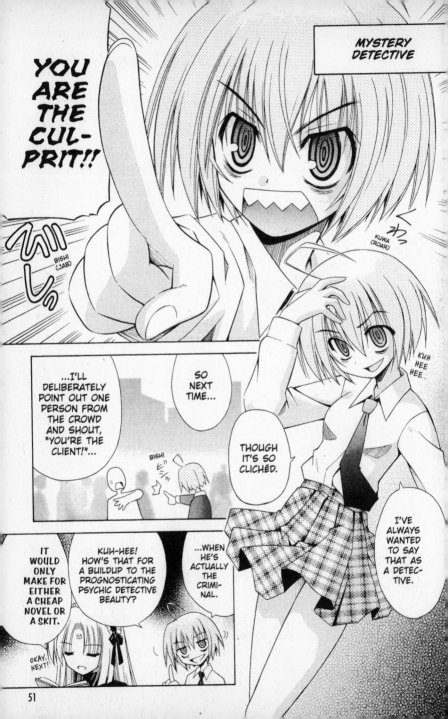

MYSTERY DETECTIVE

YOU ARE THE CULPRIT!!

BISHI (JAB)

KUWA (ROAR)

KUH HEE HEE...

...I'LL DELIBERATELY POINT OUT ONE PERSON FROM THE CROWD AND SHOUT, "YOU'RE THE CLIENT!"...

SO NEXT TIME...

THOUGH IT'S SO CLICHÉD.

BISHI

I'VE ALWAYS WANTED TO SAY THAT AS A DETECTIVE.

IT WOULD ONLY MAKE FOR EITHER A CHEAP NOVEL OR A SKIT.

KUH-HEE! HOW'S THAT FOR A BUILDUP TO THE PROGNOSTICATING PSYCHIC DETECTIVE BEAUTY?

...WHEN HE'S ACTUALLY THE CRIMINAL.

OKAY, NEXT!

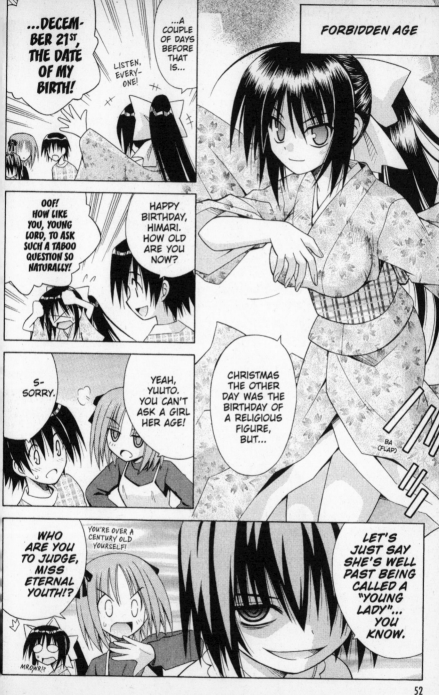

...DECEMBER 21ST, THE DATE OF MY BIRTH!

...A COUPLE OF DAYS BEFORE THAT IS...

LISTEN, EVERYONE!

FORBIDDEN AGE

OOF! HOW LIKE YOU, YOUNG LORD, TO ASK SUCH A TABOO QUESTION SO NATURALLY!

HAPPY BIRTHDAY, HIMARI. HOW OLD ARE YOU NOW?

S-SORRY.

YEAH, YUUTO. YOU CAN'T ASK A GIRL HER AGE!

CHRISTMAS THE OTHER DAY WAS THE BIRTHDAY OF A RELIGIOUS FIGURE, BUT...

BA (FLAP)

WHO ARE YOU TO JUDGE, MISS ETERNAL YOUTH!?

YOU'RE OVER A CENTURY OLD YOURSELF!

MROWR!?

LET'S JUST SAY SHE'S WELL PAST BEING CALLED A "YOUNG LADY"... YOU KNOW.

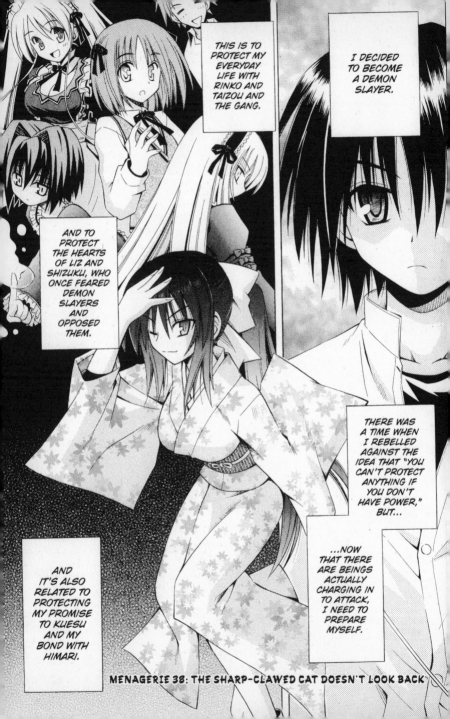

THIS IS TO PROTECT MY EVERYDAY LIFE WITH RINKO AND TAIZOU AND THE GANG.

I DECIDED TO BECOME A DEMON SLAYER.

AND TO PROTECT THE HEARTS OF LIZ AND SHIZUKU, WHO ONCE FEARED DEMON SLAYERS AND OPPOSED THEM.

THERE WAS A TIME WHEN I REBELLED AGAINST THE IDEA THAT "YOU CAN'T PROTECT ANYTHING IF YOU DON'T HAVE POWER," BUT...

...NOW THAT THERE ARE BEINGS ACTUALLY CHARGING IN TO ATTACK, I NEED TO PREPARE MYSELF.

AND IT'S ALSO RELATED TO PROTECTING MY PROMISE TO KUESU AND MY BOND WITH HIMARI.

MENAGERIE 38: THE SHARP-CLAWED CAT DOESN'T LOOK BACK

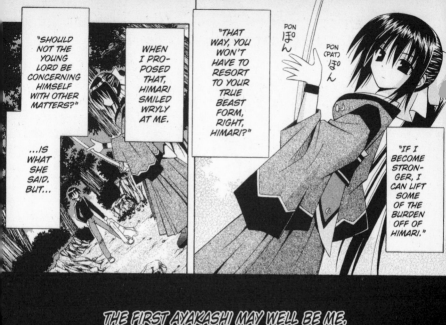

"SHOULD NOT THE YOUNG LORD BE CONCERNING HIMSELF WITH OTHER MATTERS?"

...IS WHAT SHE SAID. BUT...

WHEN I PROPOSED THAT, HIMARI SMILED WRYLY AT ME.

"THAT WAY, YOU WON'T HAVE TO RESORT TO YOUR TRUE BEAST FORM, RIGHT, HIMARI?"

PON ぽん

PON (PAT) ぽん

"IF I BECOME STRONGER, I CAN LIFT SOME OF THE BURDEN OFF OF HIMARI."

THE FIRST AYAKASHI MAY WELL BE ME.

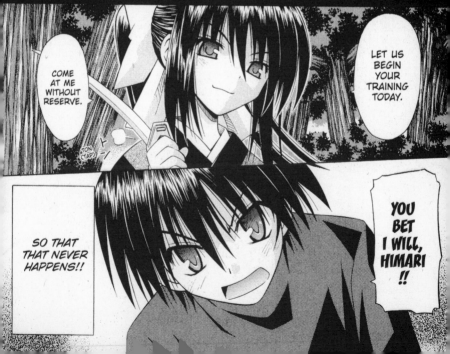

LET US BEGIN YOUR TRAINING TODAY.

COME AT ME WITHOUT RESERVE.

TON (TAP)

SO THAT THAT NEVER HAPPENS!!

YOU BET I WILL, HIMARI!!

MENAGERIE 38:
THE SHARP-CLAWED CAT DOESN'T LOOK BACK

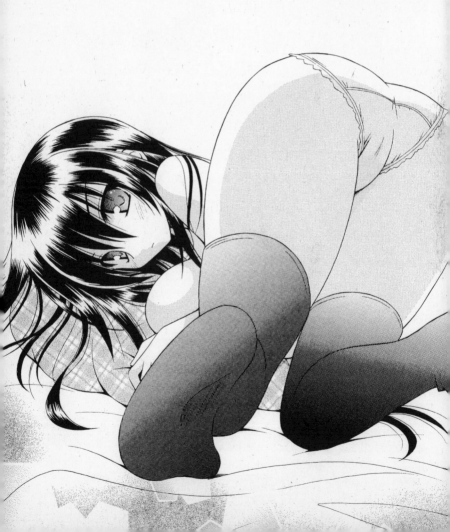

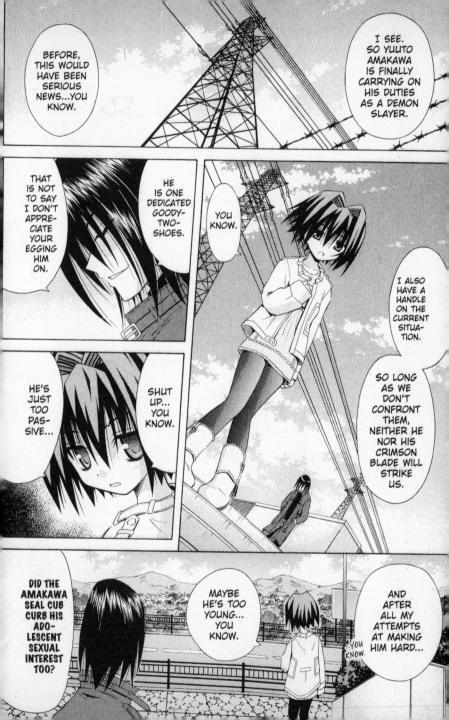

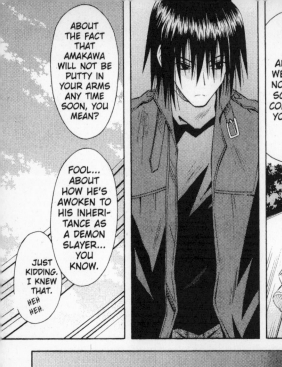

ABOUT THE FACT THAT AMAKAWA WILL NOT BE PUTTY IN YOUR ARMS ANY TIME SOON, YOU MEAN?

FOOL... ABOUT HOW HE'S AWOKEN TO HIS INHERI-TANCE AS A DEMON SLAYER... YOU KNOW.

JUST KIDDING. I KNEW THAT.

HEH HEH.

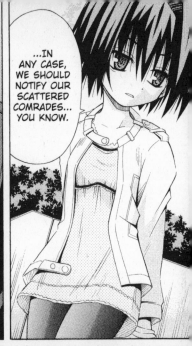

...IN ANY CASE, WE SHOULD NOTIFY OUR SCATTERED COMRADES... YOU KNOW.

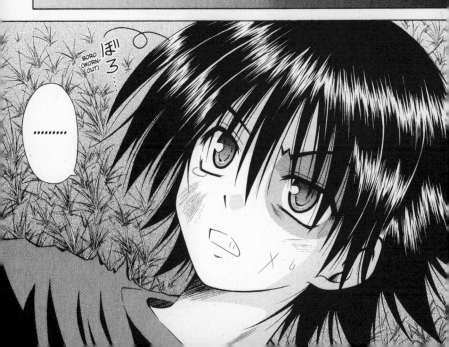

BORO (WORN-OUT)

....

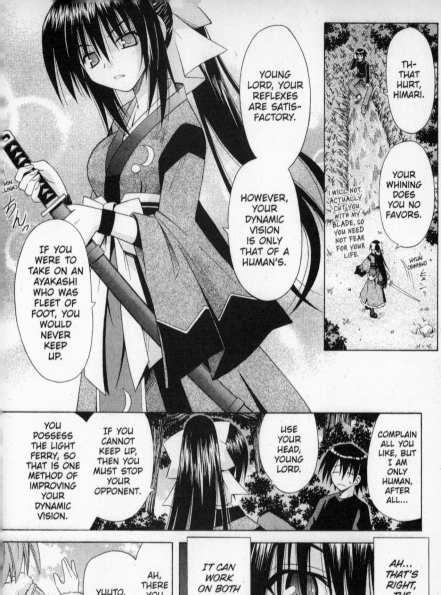

YOUNG LORD, YOUR REFLEXES ARE SATISFACTORY.

HOWEVER, YOUR DYNAMIC VISION IS ONLY THAT OF A HUMAN'S.

IF YOU WERE TO TAKE ON AN AYAKASHI WHO WAS FLEET OF FOOT, YOU WOULD NEVER KEEP UP.

TH-THAT HURT, HIMARI.

YOUR WHINING DOES YOU NO FAVORS.

I WILL NOT ACTUALLY CUT YOU WITH MY BLADE, SO YOU NEED NOT FEAR FOR YOUR LIFE.

HYUN (SWISH)

YOU POSSESS THE LIGHT FERRY, SO THAT IS ONE METHOD OF IMPROVING YOUR DYNAMIC VISION.

IF YOU CANNOT KEEP UP, THEN YOU MUST STOP YOUR OPPONENT.

USE YOUR HEAD, YOUNG LORD.

COMPLAIN ALL YOU LIKE, BUT I AM ONLY HUMAN, AFTER ALL...

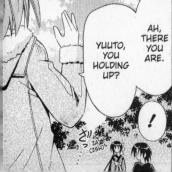

YUUTO, YOU HOLDING UP?

AH, THERE YOU ARE.

!

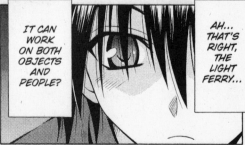

IT CAN WORK ON BOTH OBJECTS AND PEOPLE?

AH... THAT'S RIGHT, THE LIGHT FERRY...

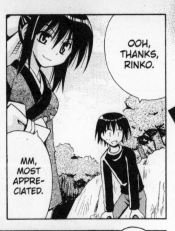

OOH, THANKS, RINKO.

MM, MOST APPRECIATED.

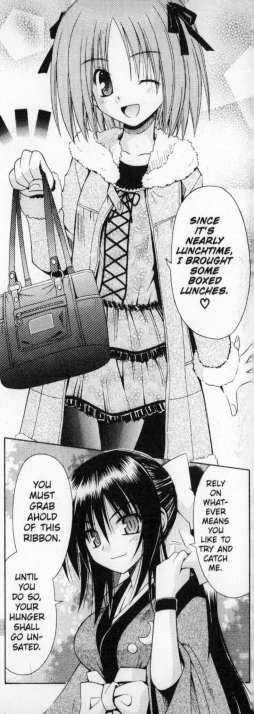

SINCE IT'S NEARLY LUNCHTIME, I BROUGHT SOME BOXED LUNCHES. ♡

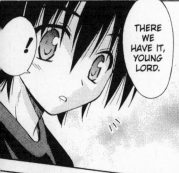

THERE WE HAVE IT, YOUNG LORD.

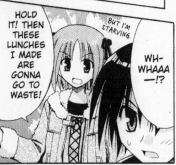

HOLD IT! THEN THESE LUNCHES I MADE ARE GONNA GO TO WASTE!

BUT I'M STARVING.

WH-WHAAA—!?

YOU MUST GRAB AHOLD OF THIS RIBBON.

UNTIL YOU DO SO, YOUR HUNGER SHALL GO UN-SATED.

RELY ON WHAT-EVER MEANS YOU LIKE TO TRY AND CATCH ME.

YEAH, WELL IT'S GONNA BE IMPOSSIBLE.

MM-HM.

...RINKO-SAN, YOU MEAN TO SAY YOU DON'T THINK I HAVE A SHOT AT ALL, HUH...?

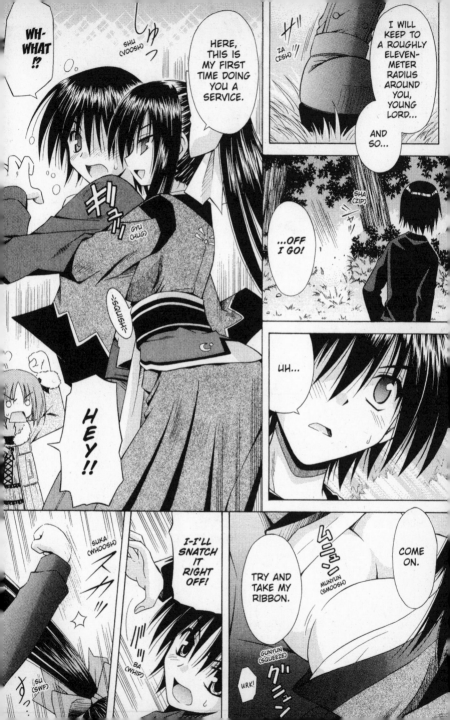

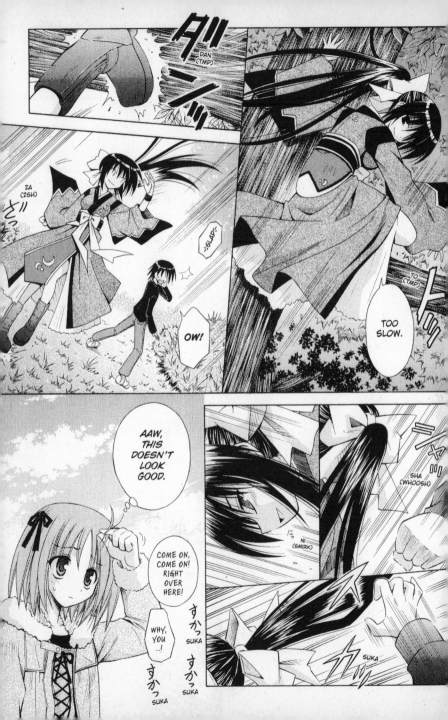

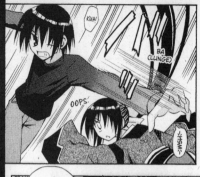

KUH!

BA (LUNGE)

OOPS.

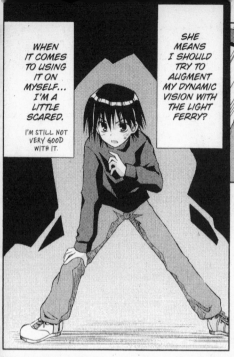

WHEN IT COMES TO USING IT ON MYSELF... I'M A LITTLE SCARED.

I'M STILL NOT VERY GOOD WITH IT.

SHE MEANS I SHOULD TRY TO AUGMENT MY DYNAMIC VISION WITH THE LIGHT FERRY?

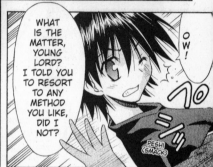

WHAT IS THE MATTER, YOUNG LORD? I TOLD YOU TO RESORT TO ANY METHOD YOU LIKE, DID I NOT?

OW!

PESHI (SMACK)

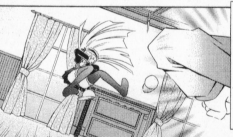

POWERING UP MY EYES, HUH...? HOW DO I KNOW I WON'T TURN THEM INTO EYE BOMBS AND BLOW THEM OUTTA MY SKULL?

LAST TIME, I FLUNG KUESU BACK BY REFLEX, BUT IT WAS COMPLETELY UNCONSCIOUS.

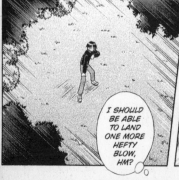

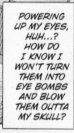

I SHOULD BE ABLE TO LAND ONE MORE HEFTY BLOW, HM?

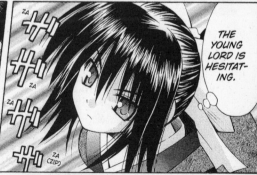

ZA

ZA

ZA

ZA (ZIP)

THE YOUNG LORD IS HESITATING.

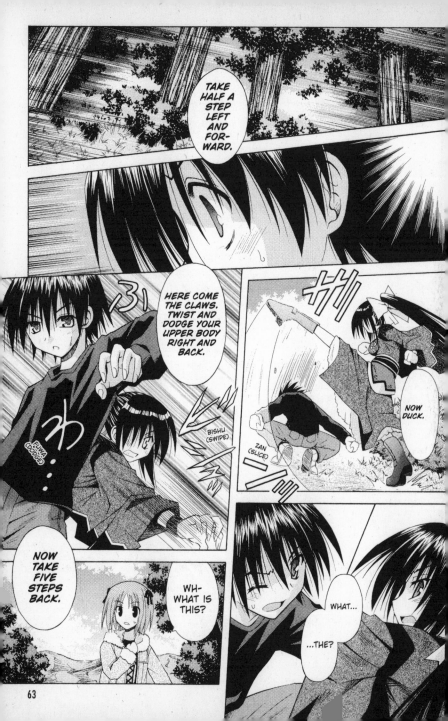

TAKE HALF A STEP LEFT AND FOR- WARD.

HERE COME THE CLAWS. TWIST AND DODGE YOUR UPPER BODY RIGHT AND BACK.

BISHU (SWIPE)

NOW DUCK.

ZAN (SLICE)

NOW TAKE FIVE STEPS BACK.

WH- WHAT IS THIS?

WHAT...

...THE?

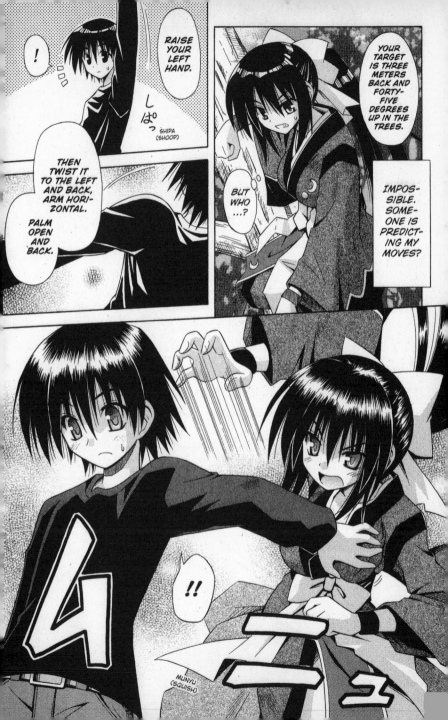

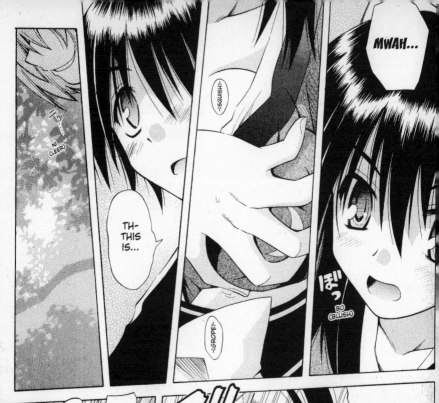

MWAH...

-*SQUISH*-

N (LEER)

TH-THIS IS...

ぼっ
BO (BLUSH)

-*GROPE*-

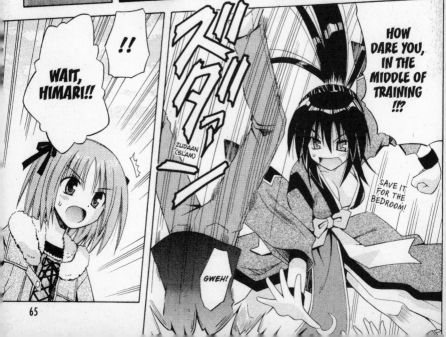

!!

WAIT, HIMARI!!

ズダァーン
ZUDAAN (SLAM)

HOW DARE YOU, IN THE MIDDLE OF TRAINING!!?

SAVE IT FOR THE BEDROOM!

GWEH!

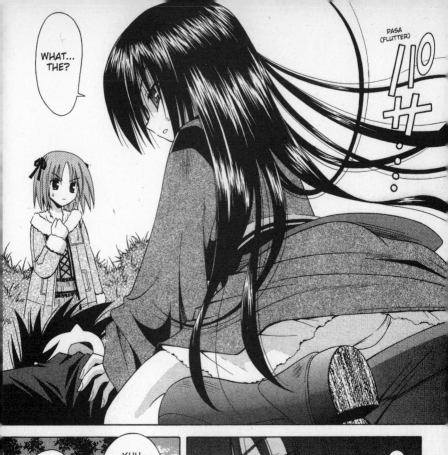

WHAT...
THE?

PASA
(FLUTTER)

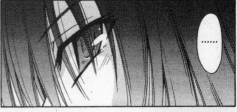

KUH-
HEE-HEE...
SPLENDID,
WELL DONE.
YOU'VE
EARNED
YOUR
LUNCH.

......

BUT
YOU HAVE
TO SPLIT
IT WITH
ME! ♡

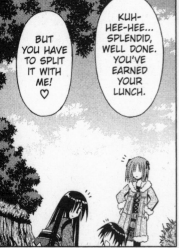

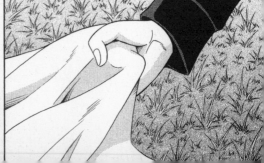

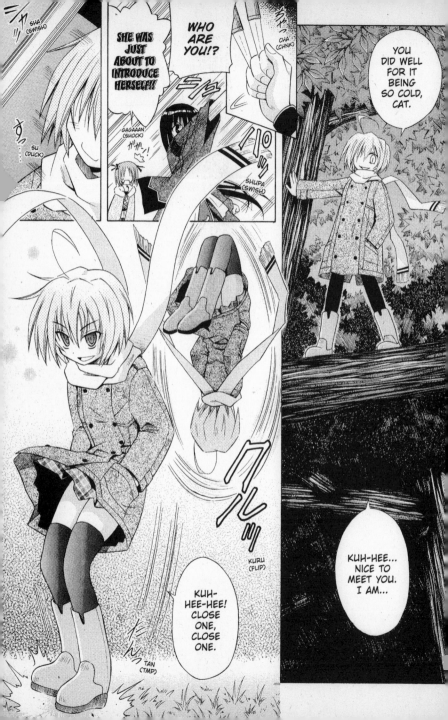

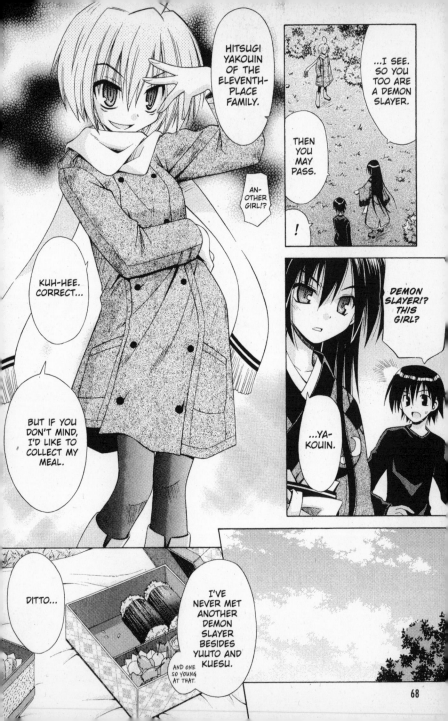

HITSUGI YAKOUIN OF THE ELEVENTH-PLACE FAMILY.

...I SEE. SO YOU TOO ARE A DEMON SLAYER.

THEN YOU MAY PASS.

AN-OTHER GIRL!?

!

KUH-HEE. CORRECT...

DEMON SLAYER!? THIS GIRL?

...YA-KOUIN.

BUT IF YOU DON'T MIND, I'D LIKE TO COLLECT MY MEAL.

DITTO...

I'VE NEVER MET ANOTHER DEMON SLAYER BESIDES YUUTO AND KUESU.

AND ONE SO YOUNG AT THAT.

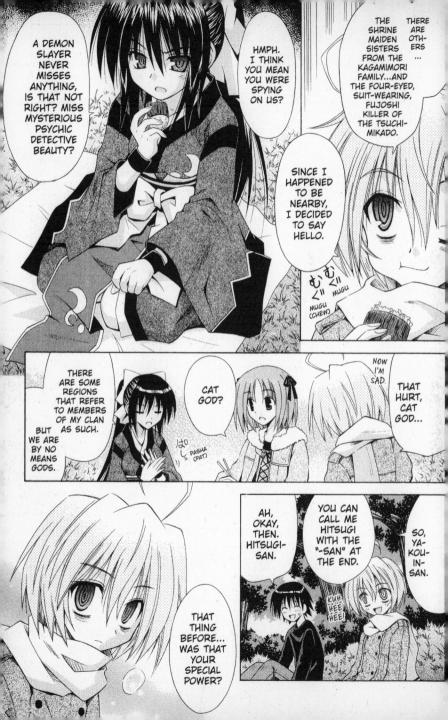

A DEMON SLAYER NEVER MISSES ANYTHING, IS THAT NOT RIGHT? MISS MYSTERIOUS PSYCHIC DETECTIVE BEAUTY?

HMPH. I THINK YOU MEAN YOU WERE SPYING ON US?

THE SHRINE MAIDEN SISTERS FROM THE KAGAMIMORI FAMILY...AND THE FOUR-EYED, SUIT-WEARING, FUJOSHI KILLER OF THE TSUCHI-MIKADO.

THERE ARE OTHERS...

SINCE I HAPPENED TO BE NEARBY, I DECIDED TO SAY HELLO.

むむ
くり くり
MUGU MUGU
MUGU CCHEW

THERE ARE SOME REGIONS THAT REFER TO MEMBERS OF MY CLAN AS SUCH. BUT WE ARE BY NO MEANS GODS.

CAT GOD?

NOW I'M SAD.

THAT HURT, CAT GOD...

はっ
し
PASHA (PAT)

AH, OKAY, THEN. HITSUGI-SAN.

YOU CAN CALL ME HITSUGI WITH THE "-SAN" AT THE END.

SO, YA-KOU-IN-SAN.

KUH HEE HEE!

THAT THING BEFORE... WAS THAT YOUR SPECIAL POWER?

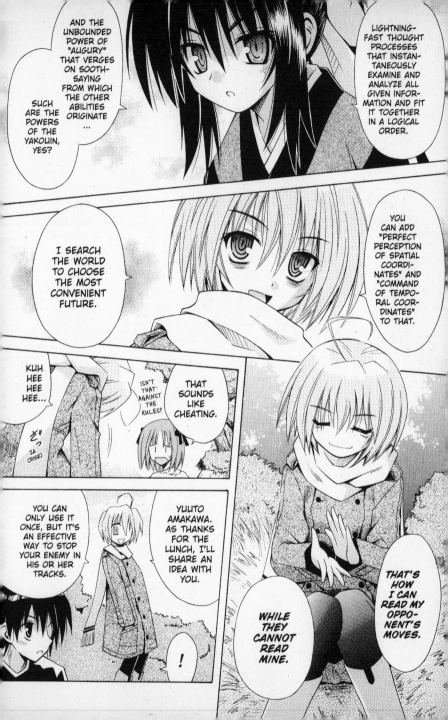

AND THE UNBOUNDED POWER OF "AUGURY" THAT VERGES ON SOOTH-SAYING FROM WHICH THE OTHER ABILITIES ORIGINATE...

SUCH ARE THE POWERS OF THE YAKOUIN, YES?

LIGHTNING-FAST THOUGHT PROCESSES THAT INSTAN-TANEOUSLY EXAMINE AND ANALYZE ALL GIVEN INFOR-MATION AND FIT IT TOGETHER IN A LOGICAL ORDER.

I SEARCH THE WORLD TO CHOOSE THE MOST CONVENIENT FUTURE.

YOU CAN ADD "PERFECT PERCEPTION OF SPATIAL COORDI-NATES" AND "COMMAND OF TEMPO-RAL COOR-DINATES" TO THAT.

KUH HEE HEE HEE...

ど"っ
ZA (RISE)

ISN'T THAT AGAINST THE RULES?

THAT SOUNDS LIKE CHEATING.

YOU CAN ONLY USE IT ONCE, BUT IT'S AN EFFECTIVE WAY TO STOP YOUR ENEMY IN HIS OR HER TRACKS.

YUUTO AMAKAWA. AS THANKS FOR THE LUNCH, I'LL SHARE AN IDEA WITH YOU.

!

WHILE THEY CANNOT READ MINE.

THAT'S HOW I CAN READ MY OPPO-NENT'S MOVES.

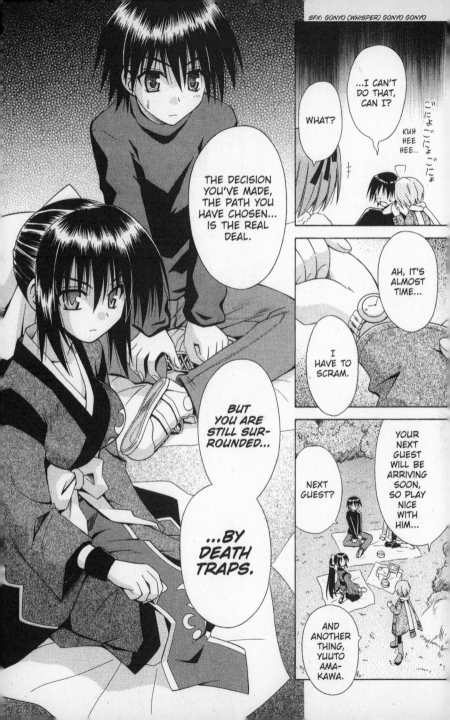

...I CAN'T DO THAT, CAN I?

WHAT?

KUH HEE HEE...

THE DECISION YOU'VE MADE, THE PATH YOU HAVE CHOSEN... IS THE REAL DEAL.

AH, IT'S ALMOST TIME...

I HAVE TO SCRAM.

BUT YOU ARE STILL SUR- ROUNDED...

YOUR NEXT GUEST WILL BE ARRIVING SOON, SO PLAY NICE WITH HIM...

NEXT GUEST?

...BY DEATH TRAPS.

AND ANOTHER THING, YUUTO AMA- KAWA.

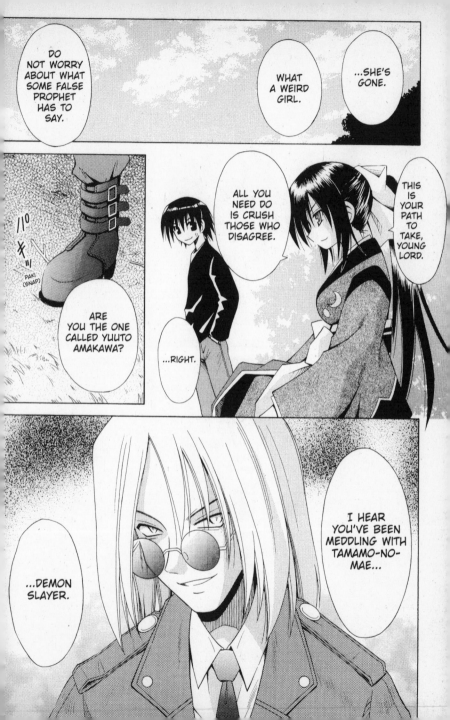

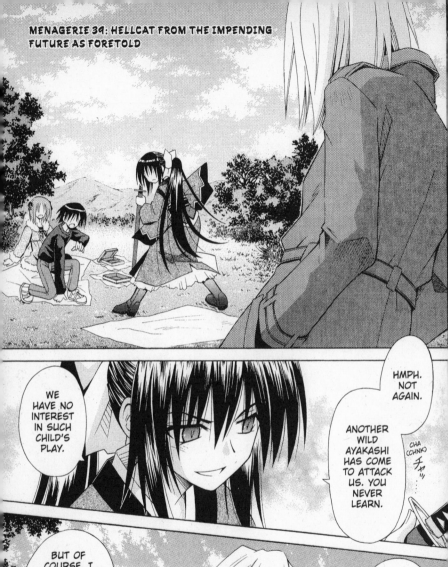

WE HAVE NO INTEREST IN SUCH CHILD'S PLAY.

HMPH. NOT AGAIN.

ANOTHER WILD AYAKASHI HAS COME TO ATTACK US. YOU NEVER LEARN.

CHA CCHNKO

BUT OF COURSE, I DON'T RELISH THE IDEA OF A WORLD WHERE AYAKASHI ARE REPRESSED BY HUMANS WHO RELY ON DEMON SLAYERS.

DON'T SAY THAT. I'M NOT ONE OF THEIR MINIONS.

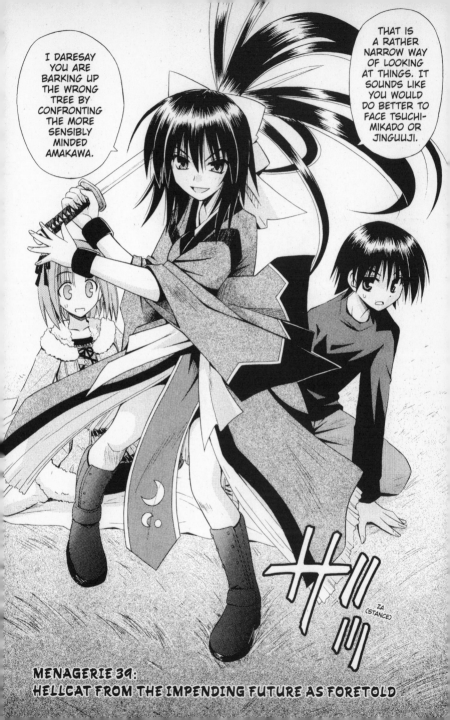

I DARESAY YOU ARE BARKING UP THE WRONG TREE BY CONFRONTING THE MORE SENSIBLY MINDED AMAKAWA.

THAT IS A RATHER NARROW WAY OF LOOKING AT THINGS. IT SOUNDS LIKE YOU WOULD DO BETTER TO FACE TSUCHIMIKADO OR JINGUUJI.

ZA
(STANCE)

MENAGERIE 39:
HELLCAT FROM THE IMPENDING FUTURE AS FORETOLD

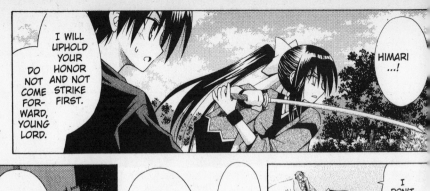

I WILL UPHOLD YOUR HONOR AND NOT STRIKE FIRST. DO NOT COME FORWARD, YOUNG LORD.

HIMARI ...!

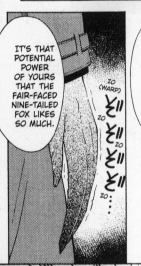

IT'S THAT POTENTIAL POWER OF YOURS THAT THE FAIR-FACED NINE-TAILED FOX LIKES SO MUCH.

ZO (WARP)
ZO
ZO
ZO
ZO
ZO...

...SURE. I DIDN'T COME HERE SO WE COULD KILL EACH OTHER.

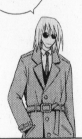

TALK IT OUT?

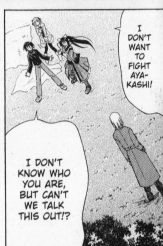

I DON'T WANT TO FIGHT AYA-KASHI!

I DON'T KNOW WHO YOU ARE, BUT CAN'T WE TALK THIS OUT!?

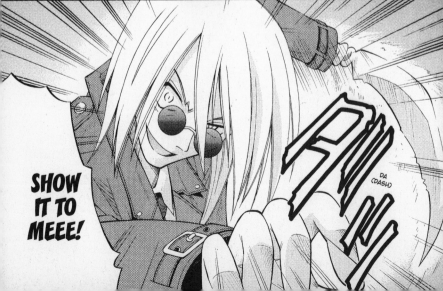

SHOW IT TO MEEE!

DA (DASH)

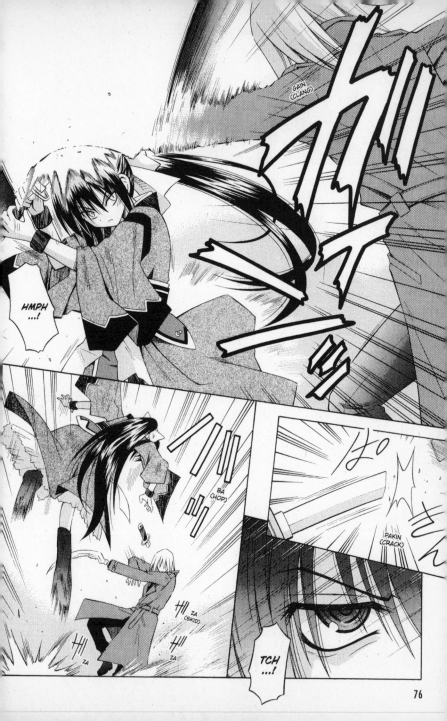

GAIN
(CLANG)

HMPH
....!

BA
(CHOP)

PAKIN
(CRACK)

ZA
(SKID)

ZA

ZA

TCH
....!

76

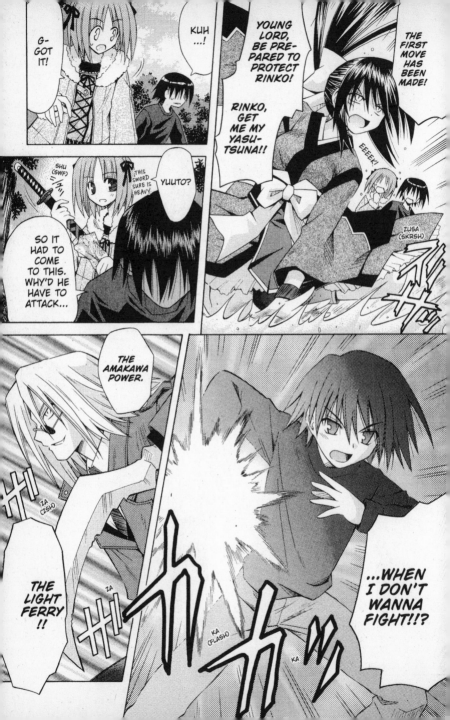

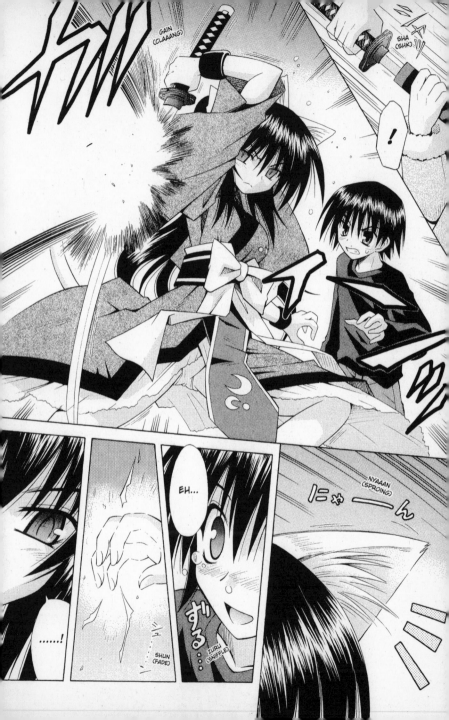

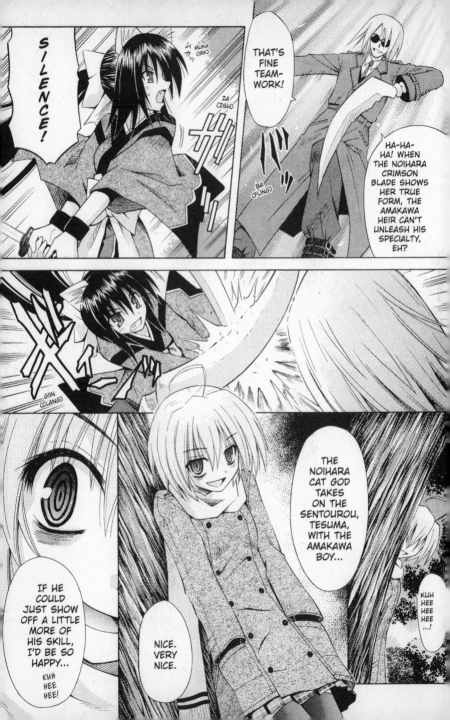

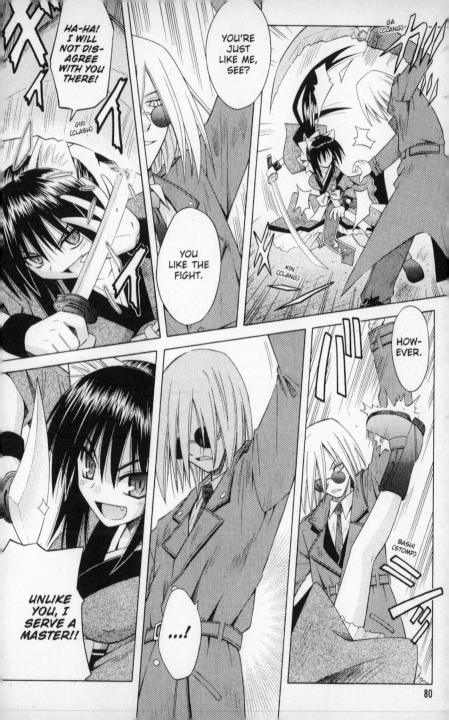

HA-HA! I WILL NOT DIS-AGREE WITH YOU THERE!

YOU'RE JUST LIKE ME, SEE?

GA (CLANG)

GIIII (CLASH)

YOU LIKE THE FIGHT.

KIN (CLANG)

HOW-EVER.

UNLIKE YOU, I SERVE A MASTER!!

....!

BASHI (STOMP)

80

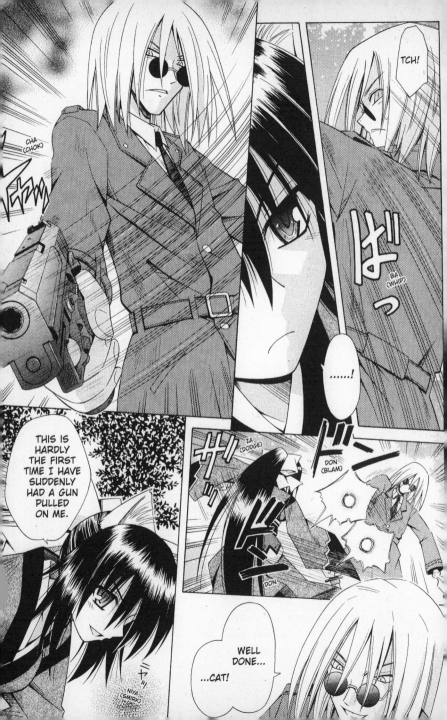

...HIMARI'S BLADE WHEN SHE LOST CONTROL!

...WAS ABLE TO STOP...

THIS CAN'T BE REAL...

WHOA! WHY'S AN AYAKASHI FIRING A GUN!!?

KA (FLASH)

Y-YUUTO!?

YOU CAN DO THIS, ME! BELIEVE IN YOUR-SELF!

MY LIGHT FERRY...

I'M ONLY HELPING THE NINE-TAILS OUT BECAUSE I WANT TO SEE THE WORLD SHE'S GOING TO CREATE.

IT'S TRUE. I SERVE NO ONE.

ZUSHAA (SKIDDD)

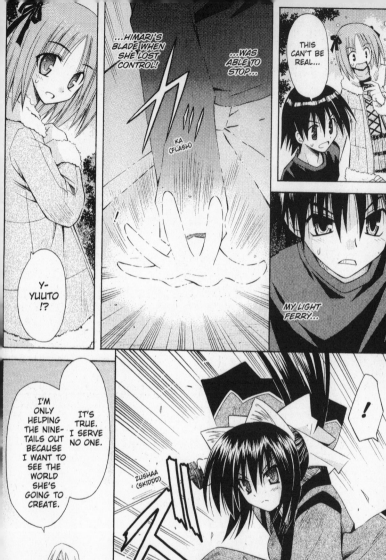

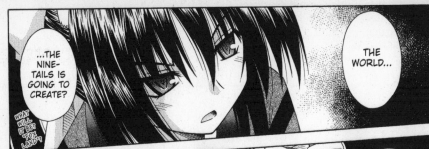

...THE NINE-TAILS IS GOING TO CREATE?

WHAT WILL IT BE? *FOX LAND?*

THE WORLD...

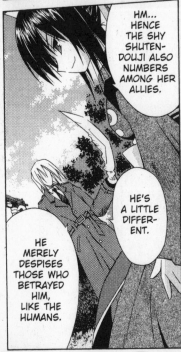

HM... HENCE THE SHY SHUTEN-DOUJI ALSO NUMBERS AMONG HER ALLIES.

HE'S A LITTLE DIFFER-ENT.

HE MERELY DESPISES THOSE WHO BETRAYED HIM, LIKE THE HUMANS.

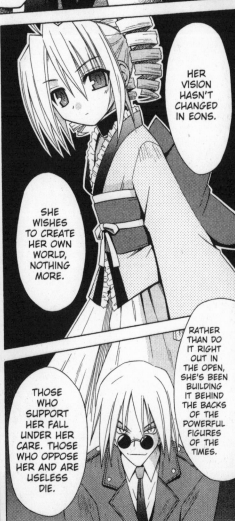

HER VISION HASN'T CHANGED IN EONS.

SHE WISHES TO CREATE HER OWN WORLD, NOTHING MORE.

RATHER THAN DO IT RIGHT OUT IN THE OPEN, SHE'S BEEN BUILDING IT BEHIND THE BACKS OF THE POWERFUL FIGURES OF THE TIMES.

THOSE WHO SUPPORT HER FALL UNDER HER CARE. THOSE WHO OPPOSE HER AND ARE USELESS DIE.

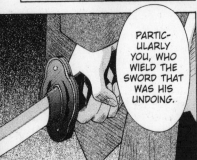

PARTIC-ULARLY YOU, WHO WIELD THE SWORD THAT WAS HIS UNDOING.

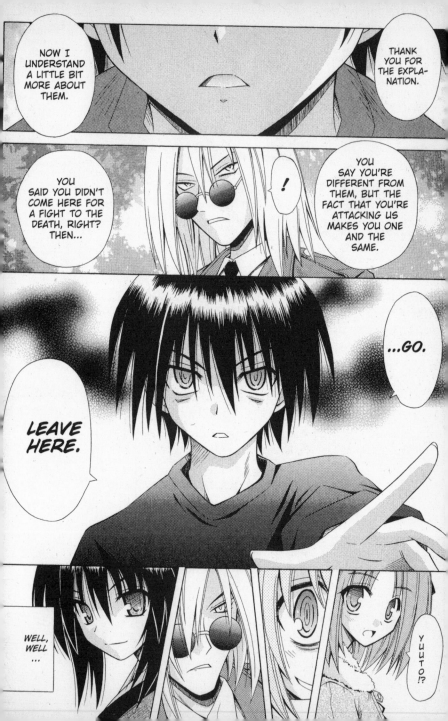

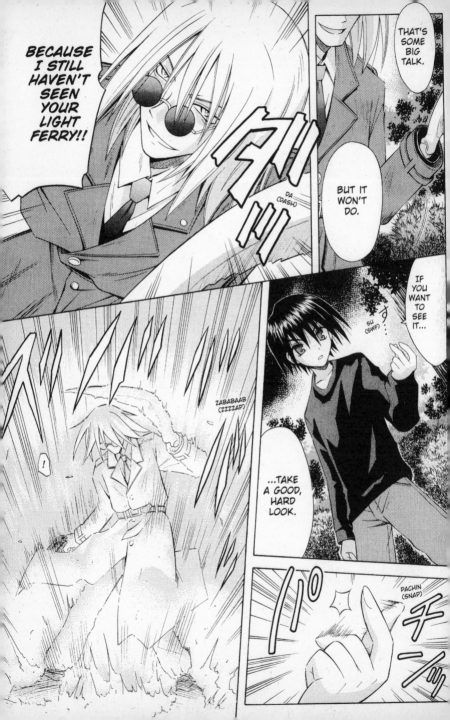

BECAUSE I STILL HAVEN'T SEEN YOUR LIGHT FERRY!!

THAT'S SOME BIG TALK.

DA
(DASH)

BUT IT WON'T DO.

IF YOU WANT TO SEE IT...

SU
(SWF)

ZABABAAB
(ZZZZAP)

...TAKE A GOOD, HARD LOOK.

PACHIN
(SNAP)

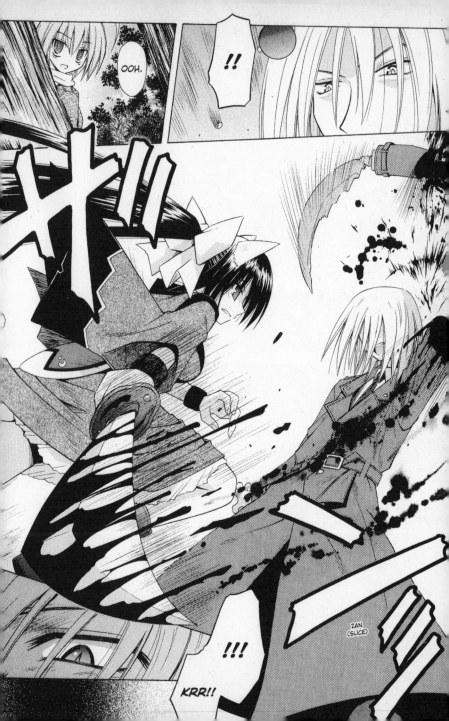

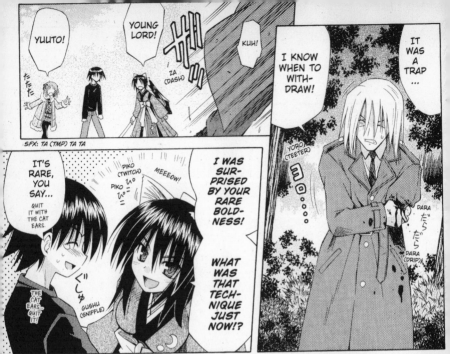

YUUTO!

YOUNG LORD!

ZA (DASH)

KUH!

I KNOW WHEN TO WITH- DRAW!

IT WAS A TRAP...

SFX: TA (TMP) TA TA

IT'S RARE, YOU SAY...

QUIT IT WITH THE CAT EARS.

PIKO (TWITCH)

PIKO

MEEEOW!

THE CAT EARS QUIT IT!

GUSHU (SNIFFLE)

I WAS SUR- PRISED BY YOUR RARE BOLD- NESS!

WHAT WAS THAT TECH- NIQUE JUST NOW!?

YORO (TEETER)

DARA (DRIP)

DARA DARA DARA

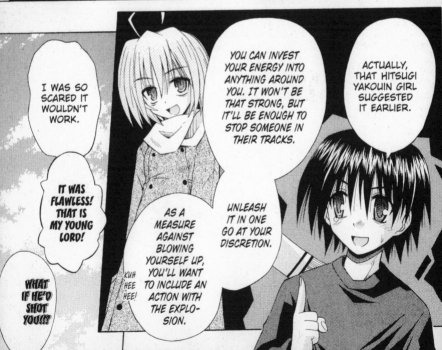

I WAS SO SCARED IT WOULDN'T WORK.

IT WAS FLAWLESS! THAT IS MY YOUNG LORD!

WHAT IF HE'D SHOT YOU!?

YOU CAN INVEST YOUR ENERGY INTO ANYTHING AROUND YOU. IT WON'T BE THAT STRONG, BUT IT'LL BE ENOUGH TO STOP SOMEONE IN THEIR TRACKS.

AS A MEASURE AGAINST BLOWING YOURSELF UP, YOU'LL WANT TO INCLUDE AN ACTION WITH THE EXPLO- SION.

UNLEASH IT IN ONE GO AT YOUR DISCRETION.

KUH HEE HEE!

ACTUALLY, THAT HITSUGI YAKOUIN GIRL SUGGESTED IT EARLIER.

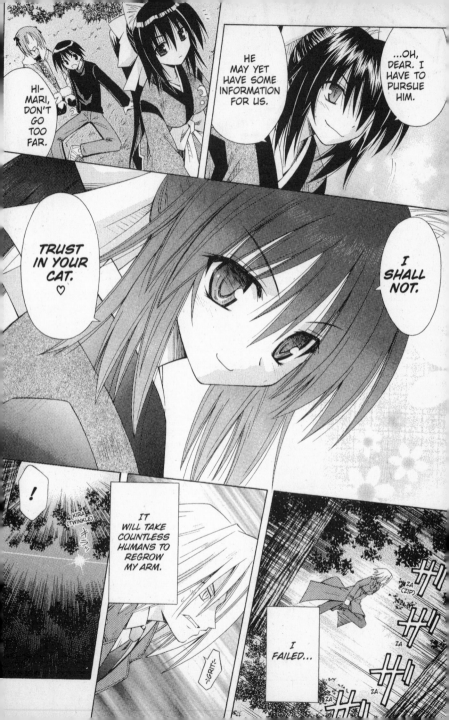

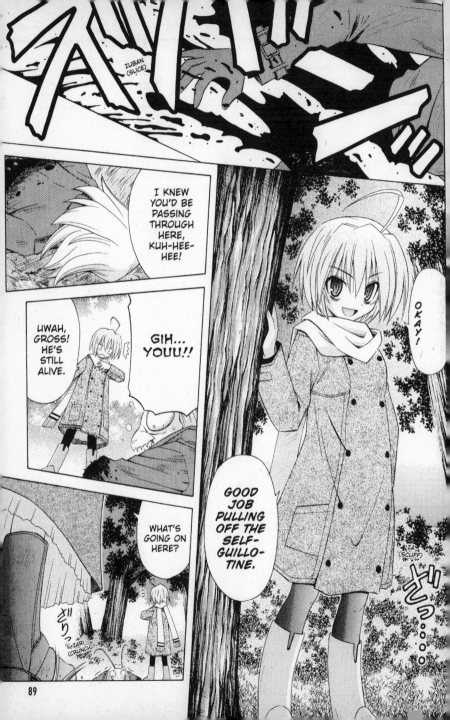

ZUBAN
(SLICE)

I KNEW YOU'D BE PASSING THROUGH HERE, KUH-HEE-HEE!

OKAY!

UWAH, GROSS! HE'S STILL ALIVE.

GIH... YOUU!!

GOOD JOB PULLING OFF THE SELF-GUILLO-TINE.

WHAT'S GOING ON HERE?

ZA
(SCUFF)

ズザ...

ザリッ
(ZARI CRUNCH)

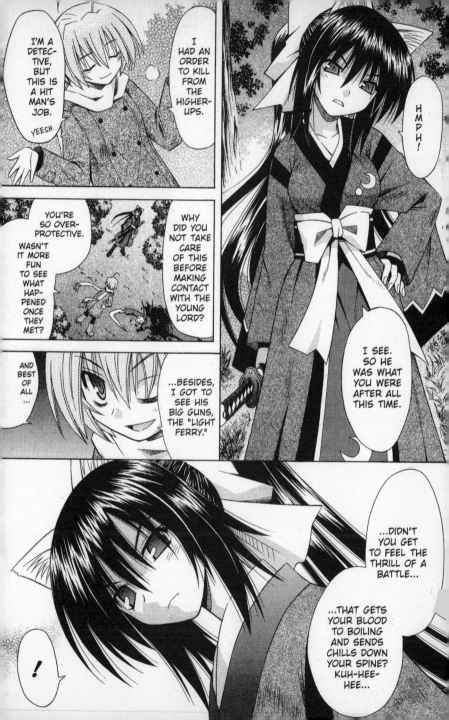

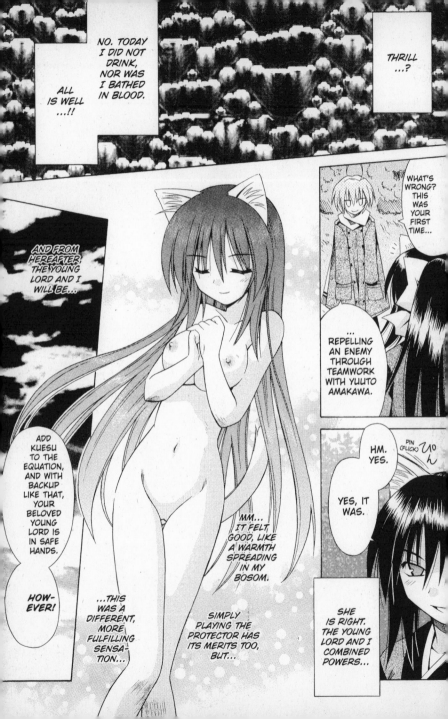

ALL IS WELL ...!!

NO. TODAY I DID NOT DRINK, NOR WAS I BATHED IN BLOOD.

THRILL ...?

WHAT'S WRONG? THIS WAS YOUR FIRST TIME...

AND FROM HEREAFTER, THE YOUNG LORD AND I WILL BE...

... REPELLING AN ENEMY THROUGH TEAMWORK WITH YUUTO AMAKAWA.

ADD KUESU TO THE EQUATION, AND WITH BACKUP LIKE THAT, YOUR BELOVED YOUNG LORD IS IN SAFE HANDS.

HM. YES.

PIN (FLICK)

YES, IT WAS.

MM... IT FELT GOOD, LIKE A WARMTH SPREADING IN MY BOSOM.

HOW-EVER!

...THIS WAS A DIFFERENT, MORE FULFILLING SENSA-TION...

SIMPLY PLAYING THE PROTECTOR HAS ITS MERITS TOO, BUT...

SHE IS RIGHT. THE YOUNG LORD AND I COMBINED POWERS...

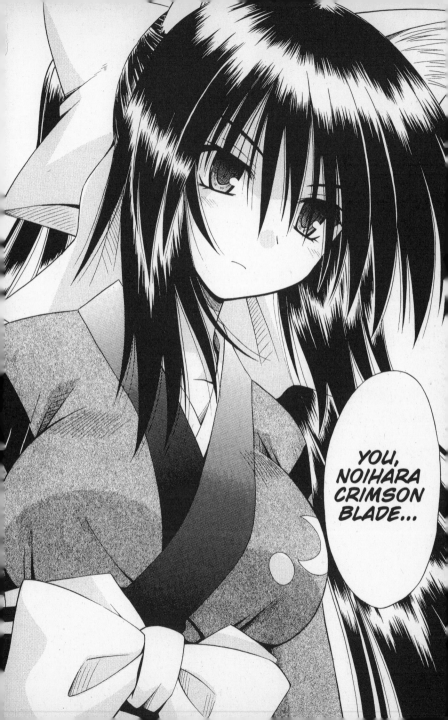

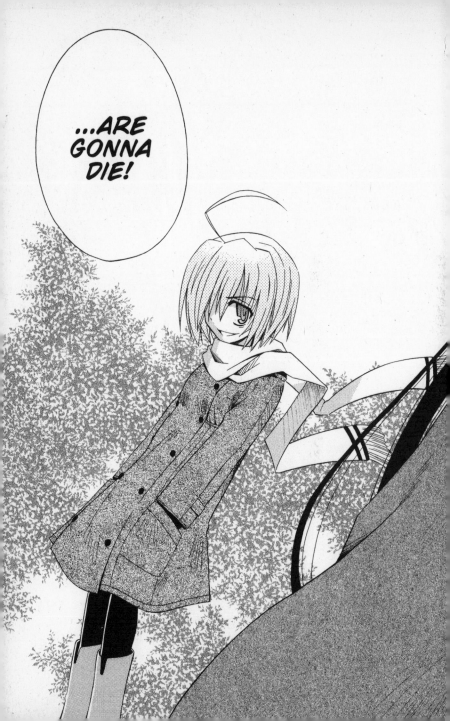

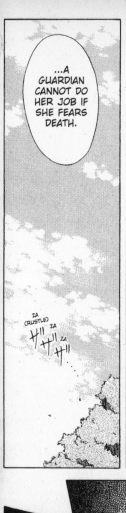

...A GUARDIAN CANNOT DO HER JOB IF SHE FEARS DEATH.

ZA
(RUSTLE)
ザ!! ザ
ザ!! ザ
ザ!!...

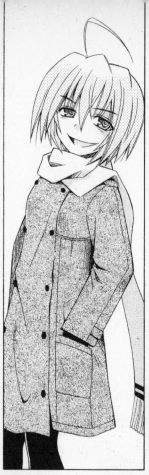

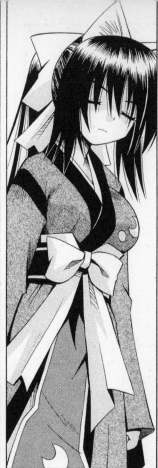

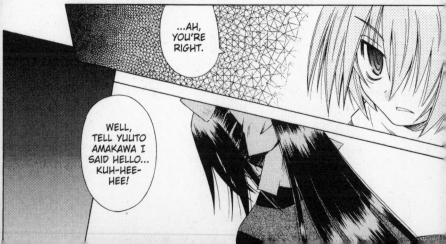

...AH, YOU'RE RIGHT.

WELL, TELL YUUTO AMAKAWA I SAID HELLO... KUH-HEE-HEE!

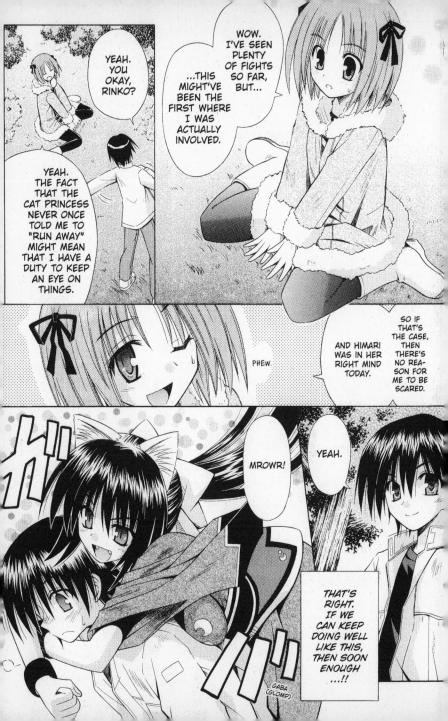

YEAH. YOU OKAY, RINKO?

YEAH. THE FACT THAT THE CAT PRINCESS NEVER ONCE TOLD ME TO "RUN AWAY" MIGHT MEAN THAT I HAVE A DUTY TO KEEP AN EYE ON THINGS.

WOW. I'VE SEEN PLENTY OF FIGHTS SO FAR, BUT...

...THIS MIGHT'VE BEEN THE FIRST WHERE I WAS ACTUALLY INVOLVED.

PHEW.

AND HIMARI WAS IN HER RIGHT MIND TODAY.

SO IF THAT'S THE CASE, THEN THERE'S NO REASON FOR ME TO BE SCARED.

MROWR!

YEAH.

THAT'S RIGHT. IF WE CAN KEEP DOING WELL LIKE THIS, THEN SOON ENOUGH ...!!

GABA (GLOMP)

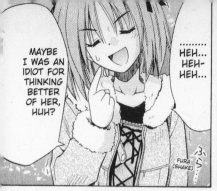

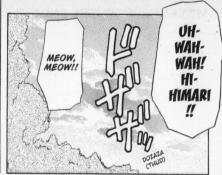

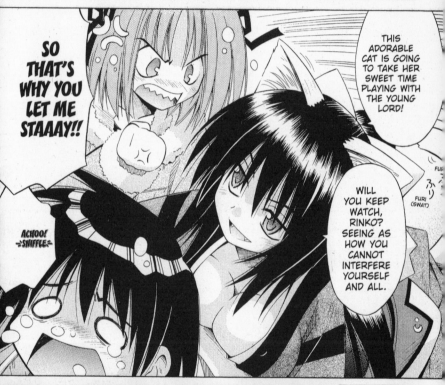

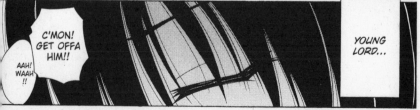

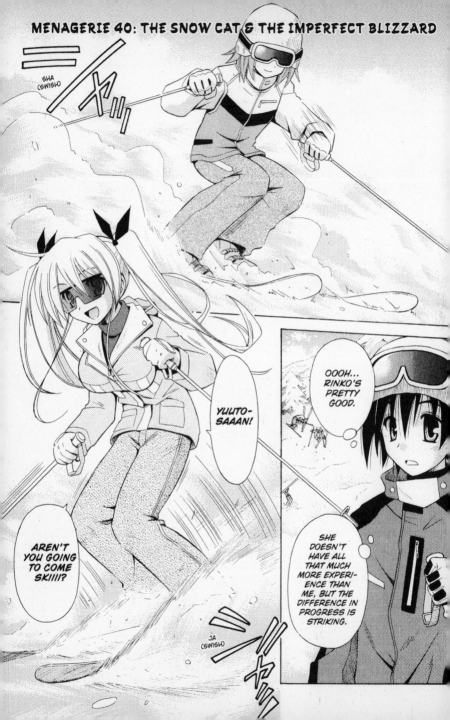

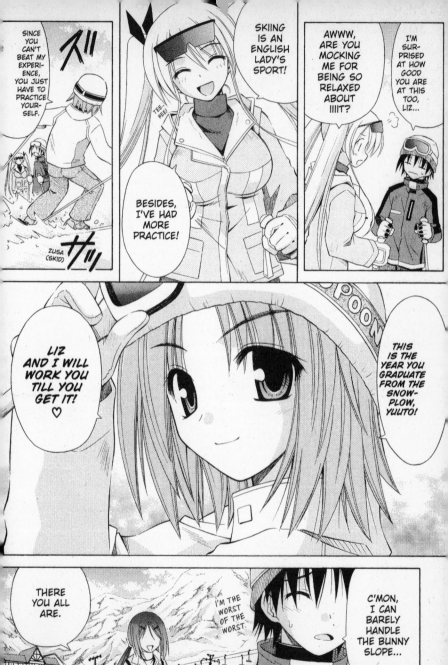

SINCE YOU CAN'T BEAT MY EXPERIENCE, YOU JUST HAVE TO PRACTICE YOURSELF.

ZUSA (SKID)

TEE HEE!

SKIING IS AN ENGLISH LADY'S SPORT!

BESIDES, I'VE HAD MORE PRACTICE!

AWWW, ARE YOU MOCKING ME FOR BEING SO RELAXED ABOUT IIIIT?

I'M SUR-PRISED AT HOW GOOD YOU ARE AT THIS TOO, LIZ...

LIZ AND I WILL WORK YOU TILL YOU GET IT! ♡

THIS IS THE YEAR YOU GRADUATE FROM THE SNOW-PLOW, YUUTO!

THERE YOU ALL ARE.

I'M THE WORST OF THE WORST.

C'MON, I CAN BARELY HANDLE THE BUNNY SLOPE...

98

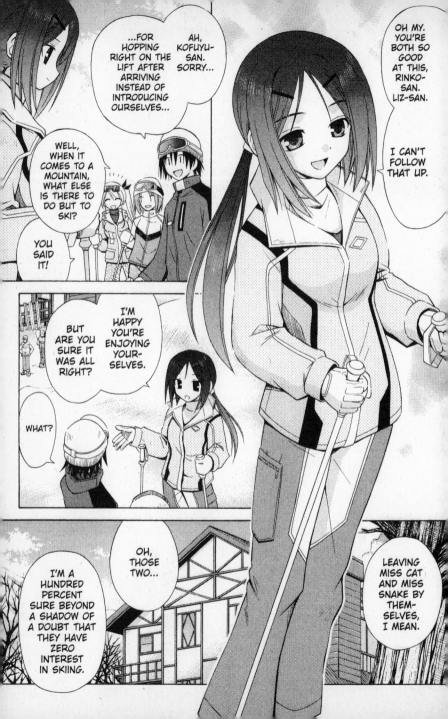

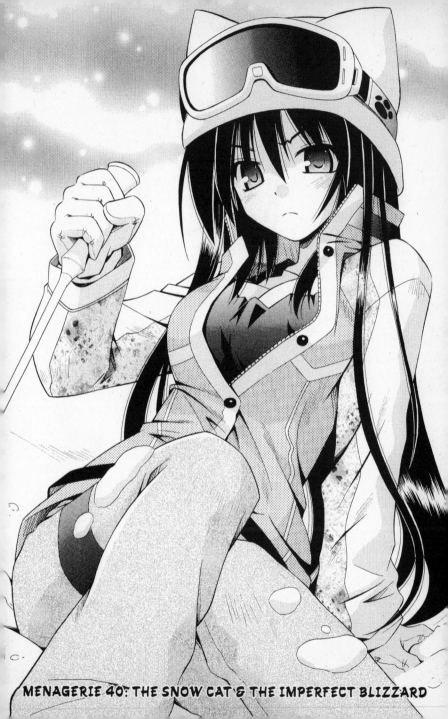

MENAGERIE 40: THE SNOW CAT & THE IMPERFECT BLIZZARD

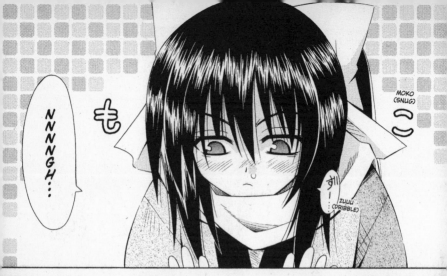

NNNNGH...

MOKO (SNUG)

ZUUU (DRIBBLE)

THE ROOT OF THIS WAS YOUR DECLARATION THAT "A FACTION OF AYAKASHI IN THE NORTHEAST WISHES TO SPEAK TO THE AMAKAWA DEMON SLAYER."

THOUGH UPON CLOSER EXAMINATION, 'TWAS ALL YOUR DOING, SHIZUKU.

YOU KNOW...

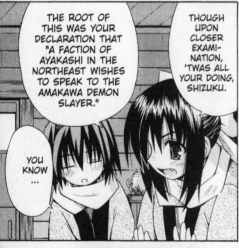

HAAAH, I DO NOT UNDERSTAND THE YOUNG LORD.

AAAH, NICE AND WARM.

PACHI

PACHI (CRACKLE)

ALTHOUGH SPRING APPROACHES, HE INSISTS ON DOING SOME FORM OF MISGUIDED PENANCE ON A SNOWY MOUNTAIN.

YOU KNOW...

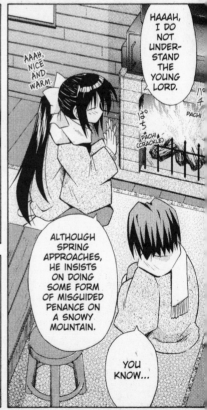

...AND KAGETSUKI TOUCHED BASE WITH THE LOCAL AYAKASHI WHEN HE HAPPENED TO COME THIS WAY...YOU KNOW.

...THE OTHER DAY, I GOT IN TOUCH WITH MY COMRADES WHO HAD SCATTERED...

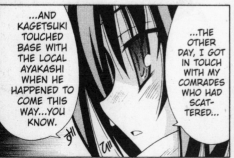

SFX: ZUBI (SNIFFLE)

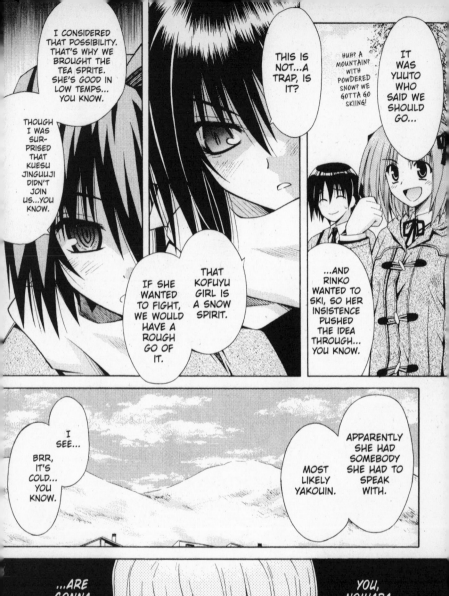

I CONSIDERED THAT POSSIBILITY. THAT'S WHY WE BROUGHT THE TEA SPRITE. SHE'S GOOD IN LOW TEMPS... YOU KNOW.

THOUGH I WAS SURPRISED THAT KUESU JINGUUJI DIDN'T JOIN US...YOU KNOW.

THIS IS NOT...A TRAP, IS IT?

HUH? A MOUNTAIN? WITH POWDERED SNOW? WE GOTTA GO SKIING!

IT WAS YUUTO WHO SAID WE SHOULD GO...

IF SHE WANTED TO FIGHT, WE WOULD HAVE A ROUGH GO OF IT.

THAT KOFUYU GIRL IS A SNOW SPIRIT.

...AND RINKO WANTED TO SKI, SO HER INSISTENCE PUSHED THE IDEA THROUGH... YOU KNOW.

I SEE... BRR, IT'S COLD... YOU KNOW.

MOST LIKELY YAKOUIN.

APPARENTLY SHE HAD SOMEBODY SHE HAD TO SPEAK WITH.

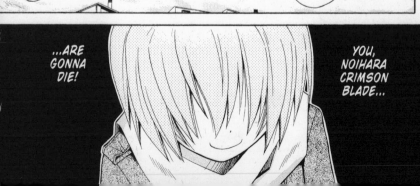

...ARE GONNA DIE!

YOU, NOIHARA CRIMSON BLADE...

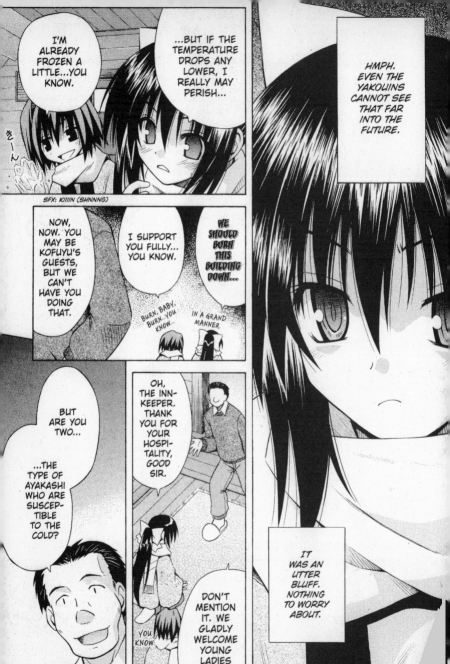

I'M ALREADY FROZEN A LITTLE...YOU KNOW.

...BUT IF THE TEMPERATURE DROPS ANY LOWER, I REALLY MAY PERISH...

HMPH. EVEN THE YAKOUINS CANNOT SEE THAT FAR INTO THE FUTURE.

SFX: KIIIIN (SHNNNG)

NOW, NOW. YOU MAY BE KOFUYU'S GUESTS, BUT WE CAN'T HAVE YOU DOING THAT.

I SUPPORT YOU FULLY... YOU KNOW.

WE SHOULD BURN THIS BUILDING DOWN...

BURN, BABY, BURN...YOU KNOW...

IN A GRAND MANNER.

BUT ARE YOU TWO...

...THE TYPE OF AYAKASHI WHO ARE SUSCEPTIBLE TO THE COLD?

OH, THE INN-KEEPER. THANK YOU FOR YOUR HOSPITALITY, GOOD SIR.

YOU KNOW.

DON'T MENTION IT. WE GLADLY WELCOME YOUNG LADIES HERE.

IT WAS AN UTTER BLUFF. NOTHING TO WORRY ABOUT.

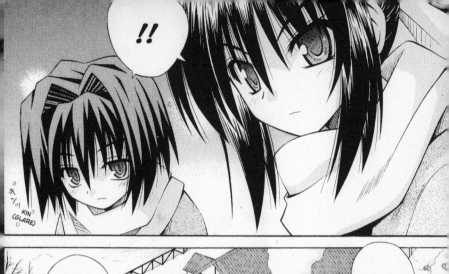

KIN
(GLARE)

!!

HUMAN, JUST WHAT ARE YOU... YOU KNOW?

INNKEEPER...

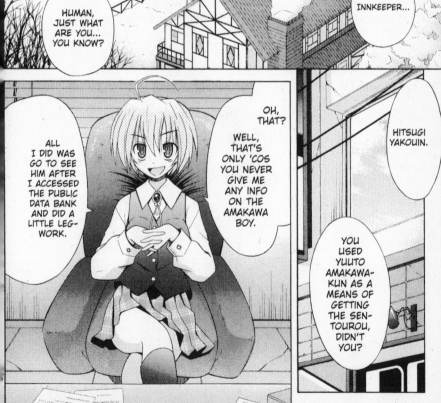

ALL I DID WAS GO TO SEE HIM AFTER I ACCESSED THE PUBLIC DATA BANK AND DID A LITTLE LEG-WORK.

OH, THAT?

WELL, THAT'S ONLY 'COS YOU NEVER GIVE ME ANY INFO ON THE AMAKAWA BOY.

HITSUGI YAKOUIN.

YOU USED YUUTO AMAKAWA-KUN AS A MEANS OF GETTING THE SEN-TOUROU, DIDN'T YOU?

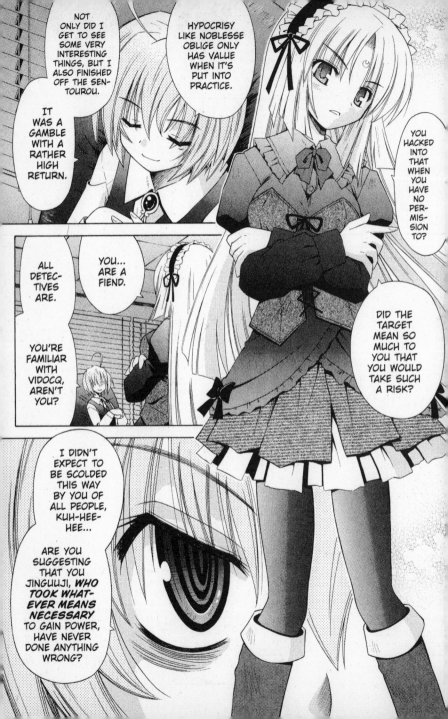

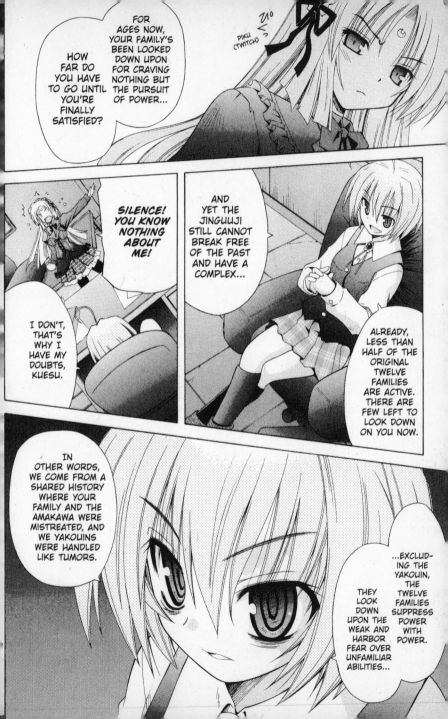

HOW FAR DO YOU HAVE TO GO UNTIL YOU'RE FINALLY SATISFIED?

FOR AGES NOW, YOUR FAMILY'S BEEN LOOKED DOWN UPON FOR CRAVING NOTHING BUT THE PURSUIT OF POWER...

PIKU (TWITCH)

AND YET THE JINGUUJI STILL CANNOT BREAK FREE OF THE PAST AND HAVE A COMPLEX...

SILENCE! YOU KNOW NOTHING ABOUT ME!

I DON'T, THAT'S WHY I HAVE MY DOUBTS, KUESU.

ALREADY, LESS THAN HALF OF THE ORIGINAL TWELVE FAMILIES ARE ACTIVE. THERE ARE FEW LEFT TO LOOK DOWN ON YOU NOW.

IN OTHER WORDS, WE COME FROM A SHARED HISTORY WHERE YOUR FAMILY AND THE AMAKAWA WERE MISTREATED, AND WE YAKOUINS WERE HANDLED LIKE TUMORS.

...EXCLUDING THE YAKOUIN, THE TWELVE FAMILIES SUPPRESS POWER WITH POWER.

THEY LOOK DOWN UPON THE WEAK AND HARBOR FEAR OVER UNFAMILIAR ABILITIES...

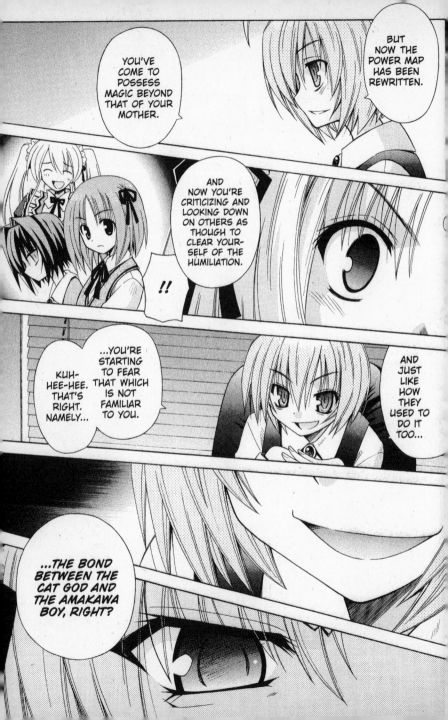

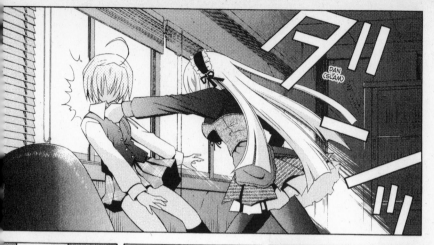

DAN
(SLAM)

...HMPH.

PLEASE BE KIND.

KUH HEE HEE. SCARY... I'M SLOW.

...IF YOU PRATTLE ON ANYMORE, I'LL SEW THAT MOUTH OF YOURS SHUT, UNDERSTAND?

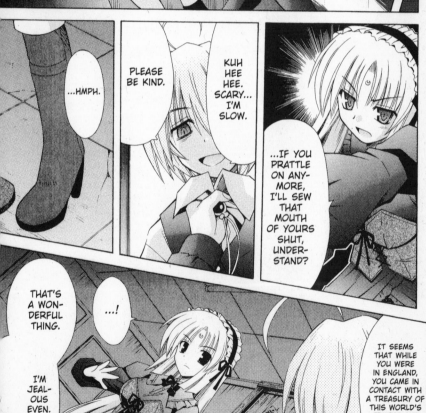

THAT'S A WONDERFUL THING.

...!

I'M JEALOUS EVEN.

IT SEEMS THAT WHILE YOU WERE IN ENGLAND, YOU CAME IN CONTACT WITH A TREASURY OF THIS WORLD'S TRUTHS AND MONUMENTAL KNOWLEDGE.

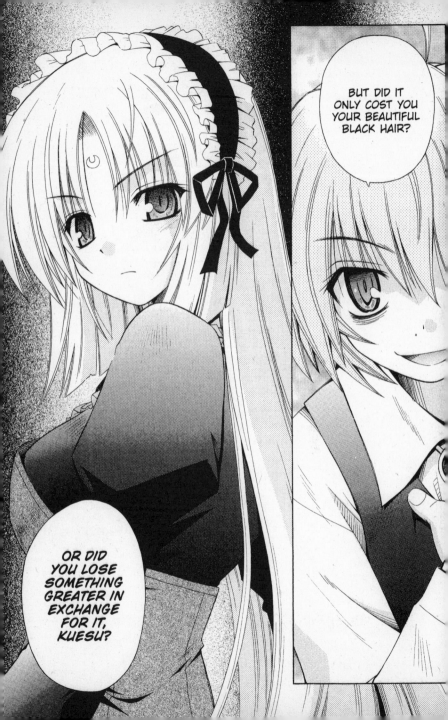

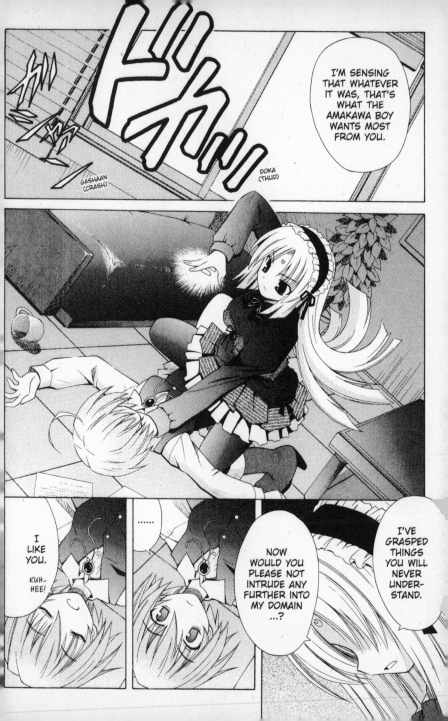

I'M SENSING THAT WHATEVER IT WAS, THAT'S WHAT THE AMAKAWA BOY WANTS MOST FROM YOU.

GASHAAN
(CRASH)

DOKA
(THUD)

I LIKE YOU.

KUH-HEE!

......

NOW WOULD YOU PLEASE NOT INTRUDE ANY FURTHER INTO MY DOMAIN ...?

I'VE GRASPED THINGS YOU WILL NEVER UNDERSTAND.

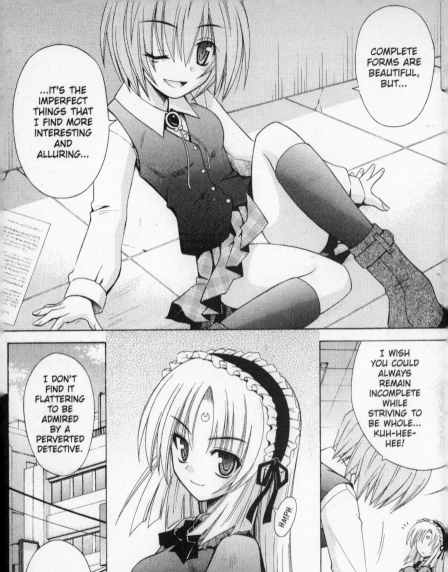

COMPLETE FORMS ARE BEAUTIFUL, BUT...

...IT'S THE IMPERFECT THINGS THAT I FIND MORE INTERESTING AND ALLURING...

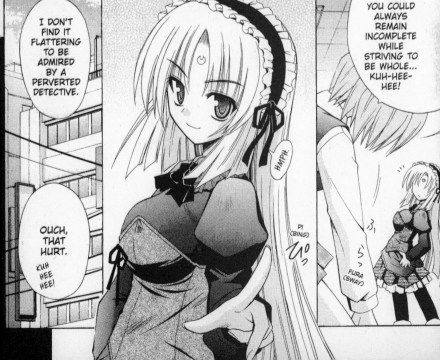

I DON'T FIND IT FLATTERING TO BE ADMIRED BY A PERVERTED DETECTIVE.

I WISH YOU COULD ALWAYS REMAIN INCOMPLETE WHILE STRIVING TO BE WHOLE... KUH-HEE-HEE!

OUCH, THAT HURT.

KUH HEE HEE!

HMPH.

PI (BING)

FURA (SWAY)

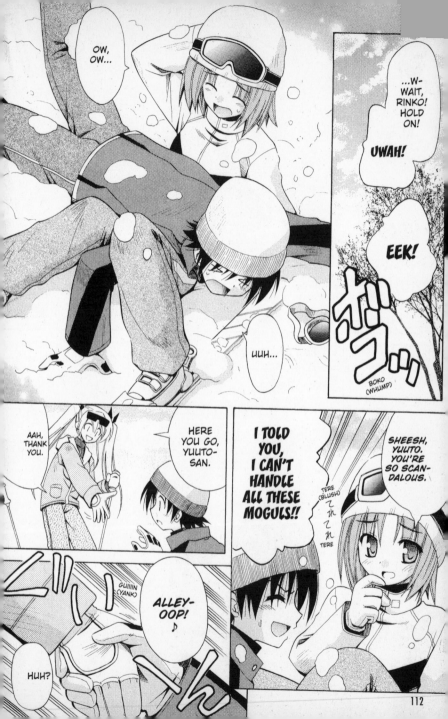

OW, OW...

...W-WAIT, RINKO! HOLD ON!

UWAH!

EEK!

UUH...

ボコッ
BOKO
(WHUMP)

AAH, THANK YOU.

HERE YOU GO, YUUTO-SAN.

I TOLD YOU, I CAN'T HANDLE ALL THESE MOGULS!!

SHEESH, YUUTO. YOU'RE SO SCANDALOUS.

TERE (BLUSH)
てれ てれ
TERE

グイイイン
GUIIIN (YANK)

ALLEY-OOP! ♪

HUH?

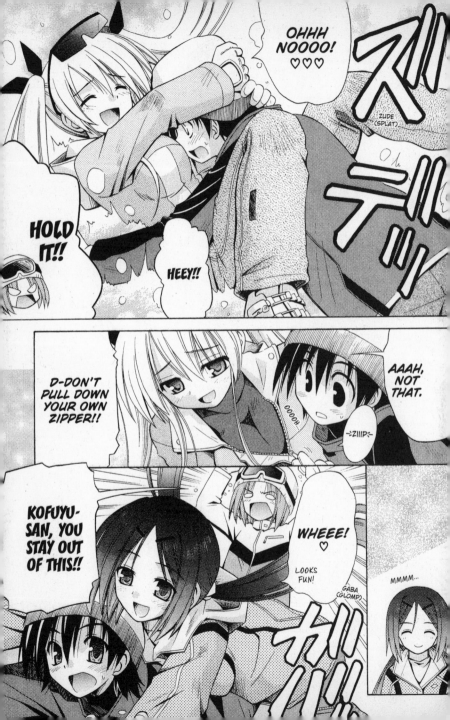

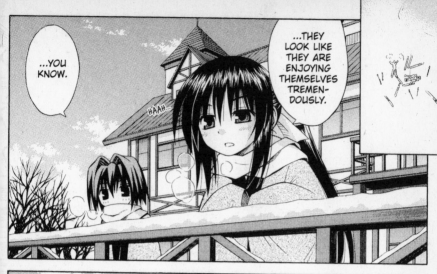

...YOU KNOW.

...THEY LOOK LIKE THEY ARE ENJOYING THEMSELVES TREMENDOUSLY.

HAAH...

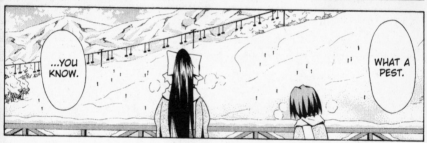

...YOU KNOW.

WHAT A PEST.

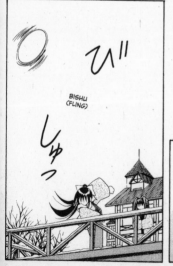

BISHU (FLING)

KYU

KYU (CLIP)

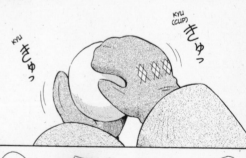

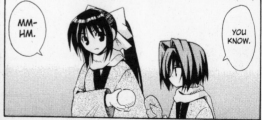

MM-HM.

YOU KNOW.

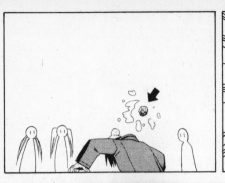

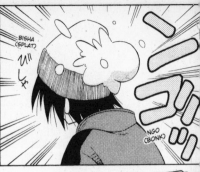
BISHA (SPLAT)

NGO (BONK)

AND EAT SOME HOT RAMEN... YOU KNOW.

LET US HIE INSIDE.

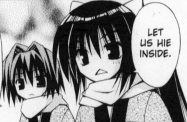

WHERE DID THAT COME FROM ...?

A-ARE YOU ALL RIIIGHT ~!!?

Y-YUUTO !?

I WISH YOU WOULD START TRUSTING US AL- READY.

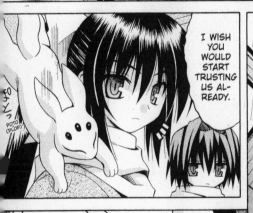
POTO (PLOP)

I HATE TO DISAP- POINT YOU, BUT THAT SNOW SPIRIT ISN'T GIVING OFF AN EVIL AURA... YOU KNOW.

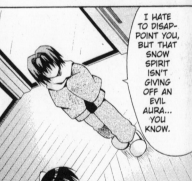

NEITHER WE NOR THE HUMAN OWNERS OF THIS LODGE MEAN TO TRICK YOU.

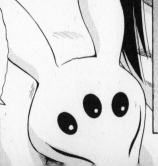

SO SHE IS NOT AN ENEMY. VERY WELL.

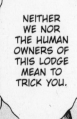

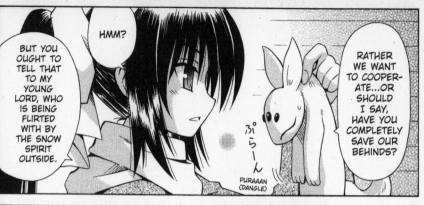

BUT YOU OUGHT TO TELL THAT TO MY YOUNG LORD, WHO IS BEING FLIRTED WITH BY THE SNOW SPIRIT OUTSIDE.

HMM?

RATHER WE WANT TO COOPER-ATE...OR SHOULD I SAY, HAVE YOU COMPLETELY SAVE OUR BEHINDS?

ぷらーーん

PURAAAN
(DANGLE)

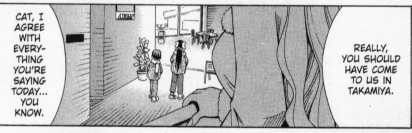

CAT, I AGREE WITH EVERY-THING YOU'RE SAYING TODAY... YOU KNOW.

REALLY, YOU SHOULD HAVE COME TO US IN TAKAMIYA.

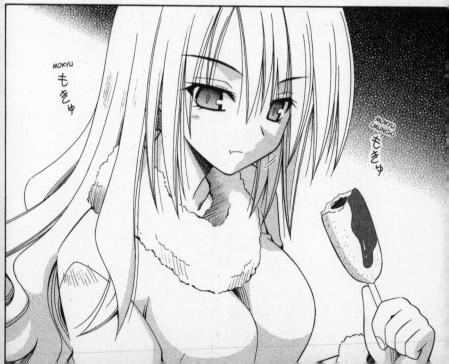

MOKYU
もきゅ

MOKYU
(MUNCH)
もきゅ

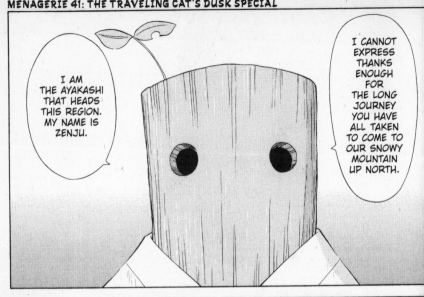

I AM THE AYAKASHI THAT HEADS THIS REGION. MY NAME IS ZENJU.

I CANNOT EXPRESS THANKS ENOUGH FOR THE LONG JOURNEY YOU HAVE ALL TAKEN TO COME TO OUR SNOWY MOUNTAIN UP NORTH.

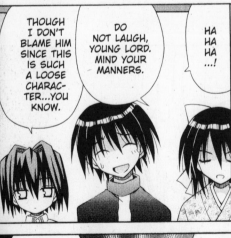

THOUGH I DON'T BLAME HIM SINCE THIS IS SUCH A LOOSE CHARAC-TER...YOU KNOW.

DO NOT LAUGH, YOUNG LORD. MIND YOUR MANNERS.

HA HA HA ...!

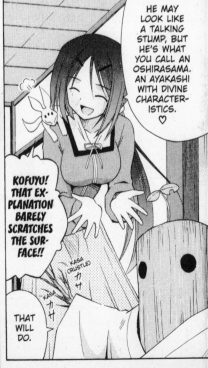

HE MAY LOOK LIKE A TALKING STUMP, BUT HE'S WHAT YOU CALL AN OSHIRASAMA. AN AYAKASHI WITH DIVINE CHARACTER-ISTICS. ♡

KOFUYU! THAT EX-PLANATION BARELY SCRATCHES THE SUR-FACE!!

THAT WILL DO.

KASA (RUSTLE)

KASA

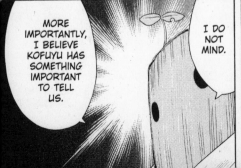

MORE IMPORTANTLY, I BELIEVE KOFUYU HAS SOMETHING IMPORTANT TO TELL US.

I DO NOT MIND.

YES. IT IS ABOUT TWO OF JAPAN'S TOP DEMONS.

TAMAMO-NO-MAE AND SHUTEN-DOUJI.

RATHER THAN STAND UP AGAINST THIS GREAT THREAT INDIVIDUALLY, WE DECIDED TO TAKE A COLLABORATIVE STANCE TO FACE THEM.

JUST SO.

THE OTHER DAY, AFTER SPEAKING WITH THE KASHA, WE RECEIVED SOME ADVICE.

HUH. I GUESS IT'S 'COS OF THE IMAGES IN THE FOLK-TALES OF THE NORTH-EAST AND HOKKAIDO AREAS, BUT...

SIMPLY PUT, SINCE WE'RE SUPER-WEAK, WE'RE ASKING FOR ALL YOUR HELP.

...I ALWAYS HAD THE IMPRESSION THAT THESE WERE STRONG AYA-KASHI.

IT'S TRUE, THERE WERE STRONG ONES.

...

YOU'RE SO AWFUL AT EXPRESSING YOURSELF!

THOUGH IT'S TRUE WE ARE WEAK.

....

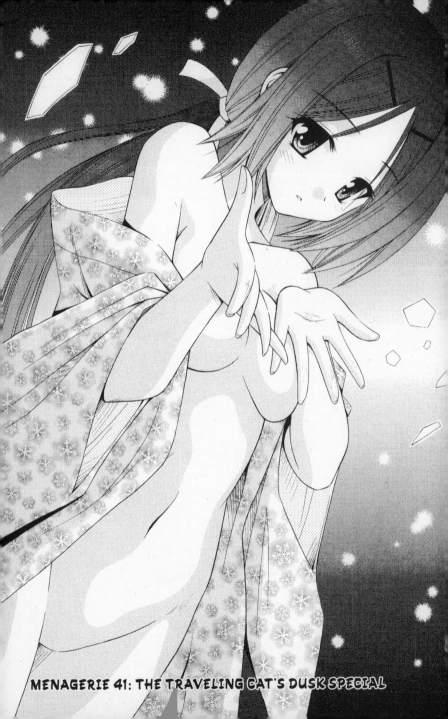

MENAGERIE 41: THE TRAVELING CAT'S DUSK SPECIAL

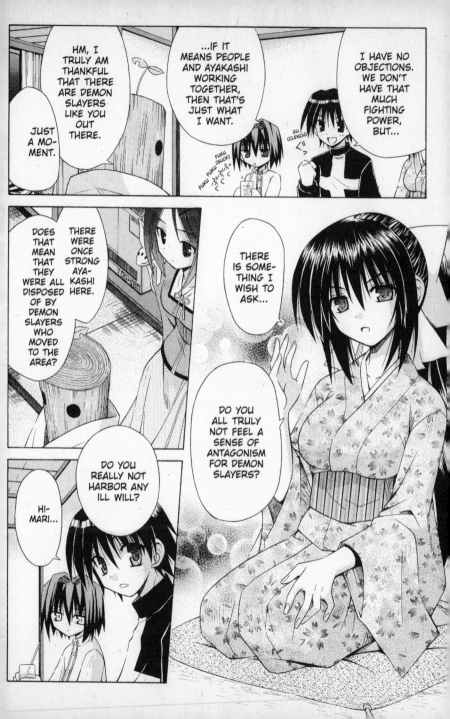

HM, I TRULY AM THANKFUL THAT THERE ARE DEMON SLAYERS LIKE YOU OUT THERE.

JUST A MO-MENT.

...IF IT MEANS PEOPLE AND AYAKASHI WORKING TOGETHER, THEN THAT'S JUST WHAT I WANT.

I HAVE NO OBJECTIONS. WE DON'T HAVE THAT MUCH FIGHTING POWER, BUT...

FUKU FUKU FUKU FUKU (SUCK)

GU (CLENCH)

DOES THAT MEAN THAT THEY WERE ALL DISPOSED OF BY DEMON SLAYERS WHO MOVED TO THE AREA?

THERE WERE ONCE STRONG AYA-KASHI HERE.

TOSHIBA

THERE IS SOME-THING I WISH TO ASK...

DO YOU ALL TRULY NOT FEEL A SENSE OF ANTAGONISM FOR DEMON SLAYERS?

DO YOU REALLY NOT HARBOR ANY ILL WILL?

HI-MARI...

HA-HA. I AGREE, CONSIDERING THE KINDS OF CONVERSATIONS YOUNG LADIES YOUR AGE HAVE.

...WERE YOU EAVESDROPPING?

SO, DID YOU GET TO TALK WITH HITSUGI YAKOUIN?

YES. MORE OR LESS.

BUT IT WAS OVER PRIVATE MATTERS, SO I'M NOT OBLIGATED TO TELL YOU THE CONTENTS OF OUR CHAT.

WHY DIDN'T YOU GO ALONG WITH THEM?

BY THE WAY, IT SEEMS YUUTO AMAKAWA-KUN AND HIS FRIENDS LEFT FOR A TRIP TO THE HOT SPRINGS.

EVEN IF I DID, THEY WOULDN'T LAST HALF A DAY.

OF COURSE NOT. I DIDN'T PLANT ANY BUGS OR CAMERAS AT HER PLACE.

WELL, I SUPPOSE THAT'S TRUE.

ACK!

MISS.

...MISS!

N-NO! I'M FINE!

I WASN'T THINKING DIRTY THOUGHTS AT ALL!

IS ANYTHING WRONG?

...MAYBE I SHOULD HAVE GONE TO THE HOT SPRINGS AFTER ALL.

...THAT REMINDS ME, I CHALLENGED THAT CAT TO SEE WHO WOULD GET THEM FIRST.

HMPH. WHEN THAT FOX AND DEMON ARE DEFEATED...

...I'LL BE ABLE TO GET AS LOVEY-DOVEY WITH YUU-CHAN AS I LIKE...

UH, IT'S A LITTLE LATE FOR THAT.

‹‹CLICK‹‹

I ONLY SAID THAT ALOUD 'COS I KNEW YOU WERE LISTENING.

THOUGHTS?

...KUH-HEE-HEE. HARDLY.

DOON (BOOOM)

IT'S JUST THAT MY OFFICE IS BEING FUMIGATED FOR RATS. KUH-HEE-HEE.

WAS ANYBODY INSIDE!?

AH, HELLO. KUESU?

WOULD YOU COME BACK HERE AND PICK ME UP?

CALL 911!

A TSUCHI-MIKADO-CRAFTED SHIKIGAMI BOMB.

I'D SAY THE DAMAGE WAS MINIMAL, WOULDN'T YOU?

SOME-BODY CALL THE POLICE!!

WH-WHAT THE—!? AN EXPLO-SION!?

SFX: OOOOO (WHOOOO)

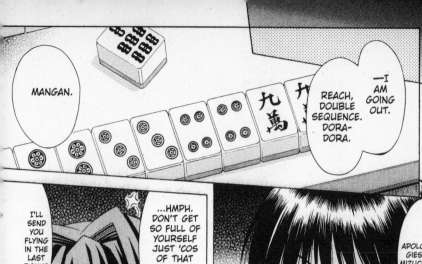

MANGAN.

REACH, DOUBLE SEQUENCE. DORA-DORA.

—I AM GOING OUT.

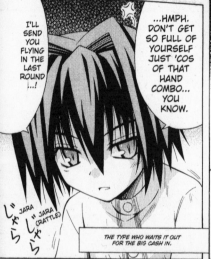

...HMPH. DON'T GET SO FULL OF YOURSELF JUST 'COS OF THAT HAND COMBO... YOU KNOW.

I'LL SEND YOU FLYING IN THE LAST ROUND ...!

じゃら JARA じゃら JARA (RATTLE)

THE TYPE WHO WAITS IT OUT FOR THE BIG CASH IN.

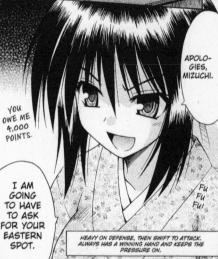

APOLO-GIES, MIZUCHI.

YOU OWE ME 4,000 POINTS.

I AM GOING TO HAVE TO ASK FOR YOUR EASTERN SPOT.

Fu Fu Fu

HEAVY ON DEFENSE, THEN SWIFT TO ATTACK. ALWAYS HAS A WINNING HAND AND KEEPS THE PRESSURE ON.

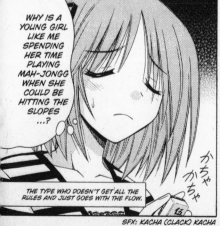

WHY IS A YOUNG GIRL LIKE ME SPENDING HER TIME PLAYING MAH-JONGG WHEN SHE COULD BE HITTING THE SLOPES ...?

かちゃ かちゃ

THE TYPE WHO DOESN'T GET ALL THE RULES AND JUST GOES WITH THE FLOW.

SFX: KACHA (CLACK) KACHA

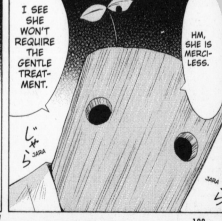

I SEE SHE WON'T REQUIRE THE GENTLE TREAT-MENT.

HM, SHE IS MERCI-LESS.

じゃら JARA

JARA

128

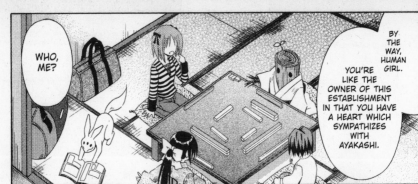

BY THE WAY, HUMAN GIRL... YOU'RE LIKE THE OWNER OF THIS ESTABLISHMENT IN THAT YOU HAVE A HEART WHICH SYMPATHIZES WITH AYAKASHI.

WHO, ME?

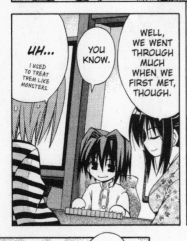

WELL, SOME STUFF HAD TO HAPPEN FIRST...

BEFORE I KNEW IT, I GUESS MY ABILITY TO ADAPT JUST KICKED IN.

I DON'T NEED THIS ONE.

WELL, WE WENT THROUGH MUCH WHEN WE FIRST MET, THOUGH.

YOU KNOW.

UH...
I USED TO TREAT THEM LIKE MONSTERS.

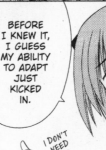

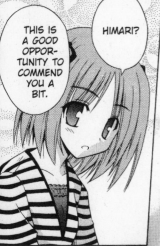

THIS IS A GOOD OPPORTUNITY TO COMMEND YOU A BIT.

HIMARI?

...WITHOUT YOU TOO, RINKO, I WOULD NOT HAVE ADJUSTED TO LIFE IN TAKAMIYA AS MUCH AS I HAVE.

BUT EVEN IF I HAD THE YOUNG LORD...

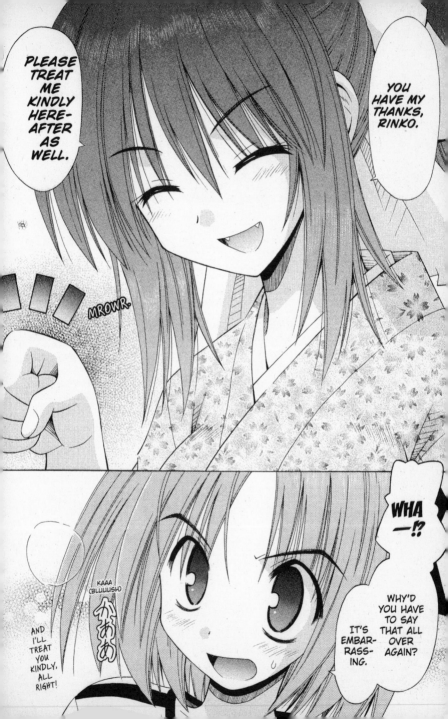

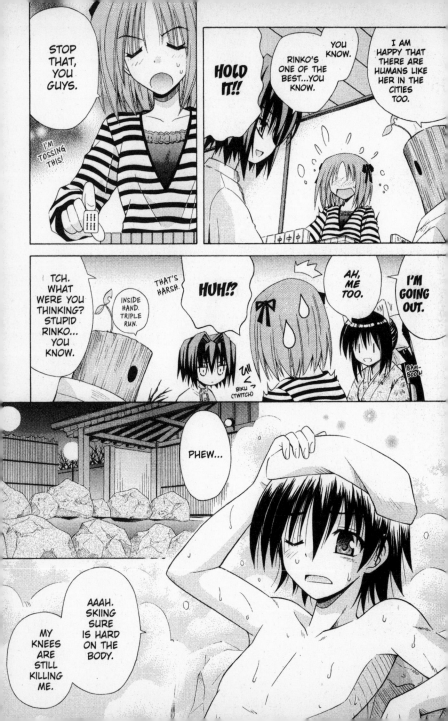

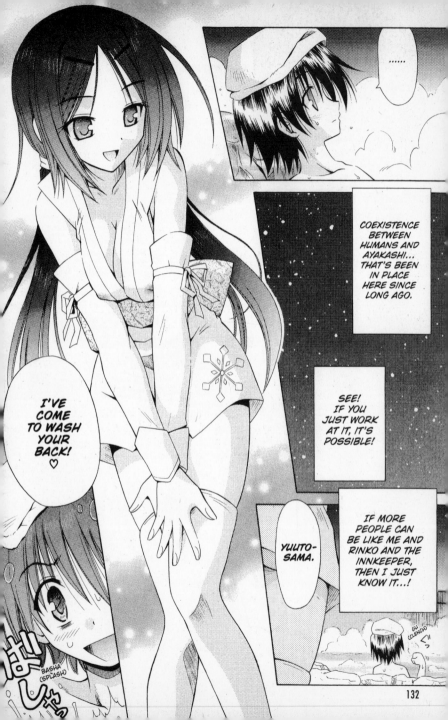

......

COEXISTENCE BETWEEN HUMANS AND AYAKASHI... THAT'S BEEN IN PLACE HERE SINCE LONG AGO.

SEE! IF YOU JUST WORK AT IT, IT'S POSSIBLE!

I'VE COME TO WASH YOUR BACK! ♥

IF MORE PEOPLE CAN BE LIKE ME AND RINKO AND THE INNKEEPER, THEN I JUST KNOW IT...!

YUUTO-SAMA.

GLU (GLENGU)

BASHA (SPLASH)

132

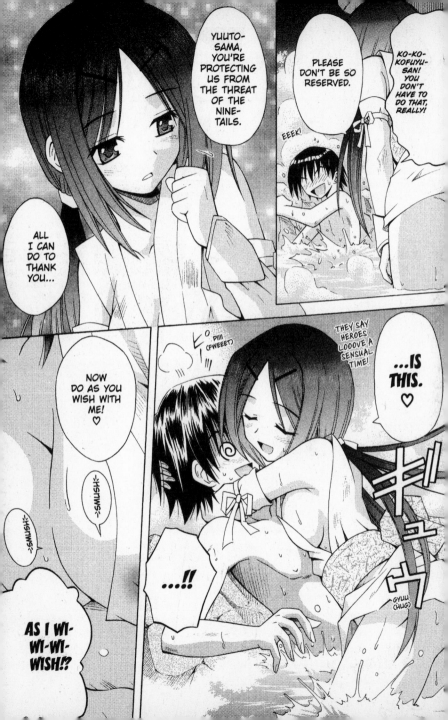

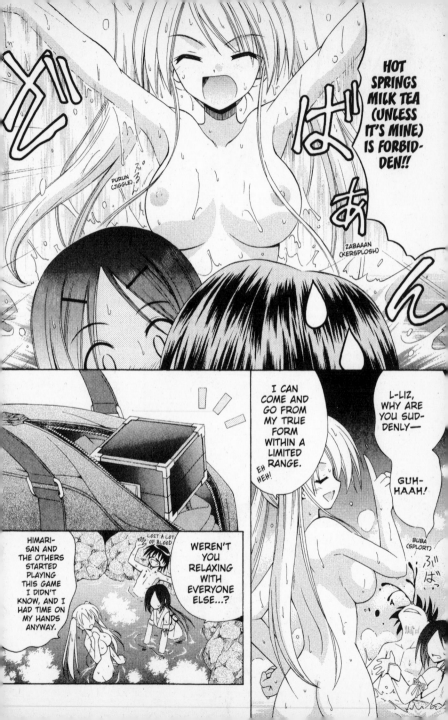

HOT SPRINGS MILK TEA (UNLESS IT'S MINE) IS FORBIDDEN!!

ズバ

バン

ん

PURUN (JIGGLE)

ZABAAAN (KERSPLOSH)

I CAN COME AND GO FROM MY TRUE FORM WITHIN A LIMITED RANGE.

EH HEH!

L-LIZ, WHY ARE YOU SUD-DENLY—

GUH-HAAH!

BUBA (SPLORT)

HIMARI-SAN AND THE OTHERS STARTED PLAYING THIS GAME I DIDN'T KNOW, AND I HAD TIME ON MY HANDS ANYWAY.

LOST A LOT OF BLOOD

WEREN'T YOU RELAXING WITH EVERYONE ELSE...?

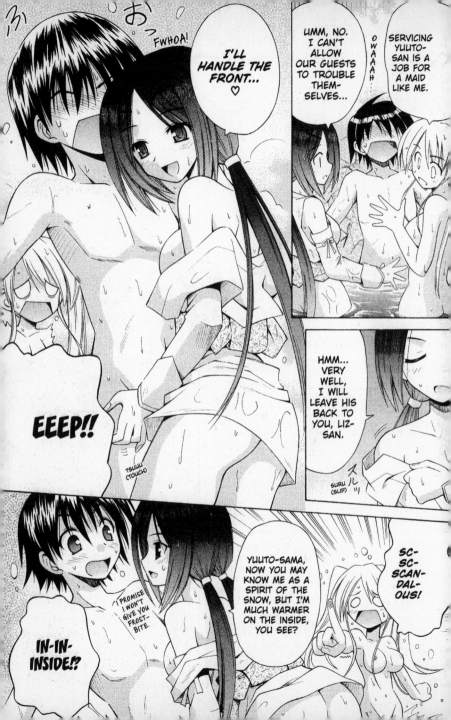

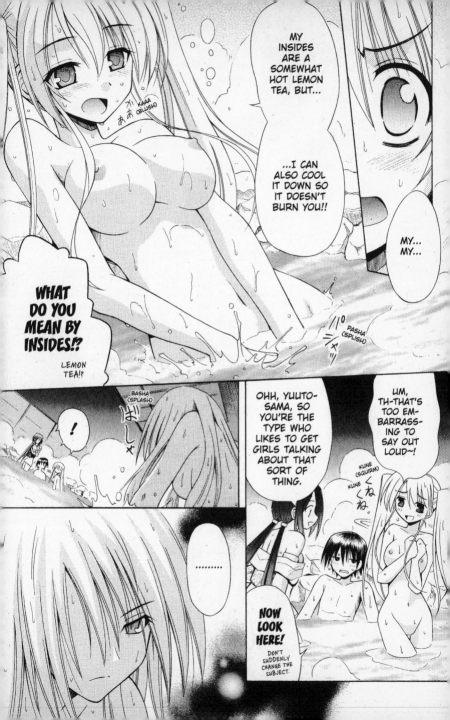

MY INSIDES ARE A SOMEWHAT HOT LEMON TEA, BUT...

...I CAN ALSO COOL IT DOWN SO IT DOESN'T BURN YOU!!

MY... MY...

KAAA (BLUSH)
あぁあ

WHAT DO YOU MEAN BY INSIDES!?

LEMON TEA!?

PASHA (SPLISH)

BASHA (SPLASH)

!

OHH, YUUTO-SAMA, SO YOU'RE THE TYPE WHO LIKES TO GET GIRLS TALKING ABOUT THAT SORT OF THING.

UM, TH-THAT'S TOO EM-BARRASS-ING TO SAY OUT LOUD~!

KUNE (SQUIRM)
KUNE くね
くね

....

NOW LOOK HERE!

DON'T SUDDENLY CHANGE THE SUBJECT.

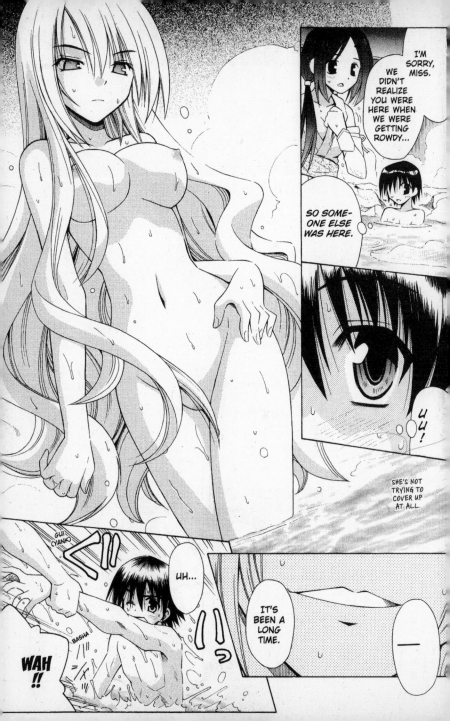

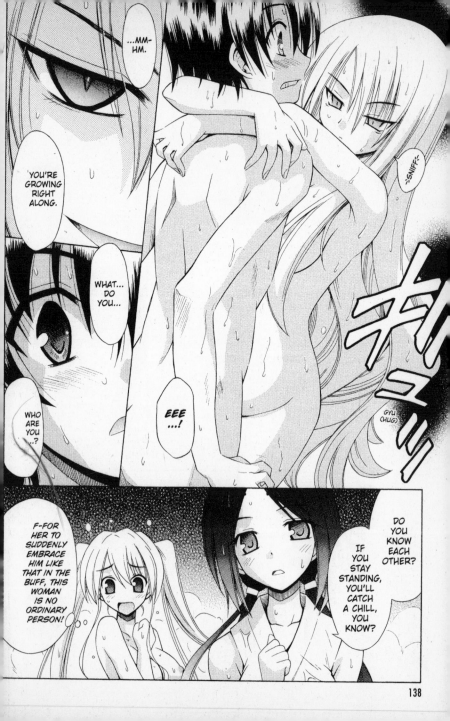

...MM-HM.

YOU'RE GROWING RIGHT ALONG.

WHAT... DO YOU...

WHO ARE YOU...?

EEE ...!

SNIFF

GYU (HUG)

F-FOR HER TO SUDDENLY EMBRACE HIM LIKE THAT IN THE BUFF, THIS WOMAN IS NO ORDINARY PERSON!

IF YOU STAY STANDING, YOU'LL CATCH A CHILL, YOU KNOW?

DO YOU KNOW EACH OTHER?

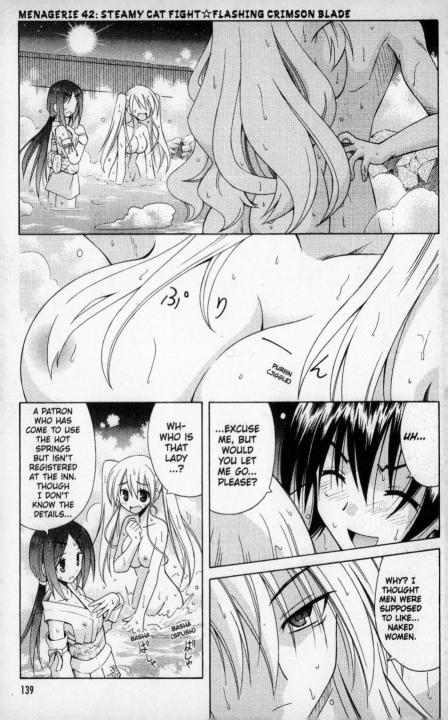

PURIIIN
(JIGGLE)

A PATRON WHO HAS COME TO USE THE HOT SPRINGS BUT ISN'T REGISTERED AT THE INN. THOUGH I DON'T KNOW THE DETAILS...

WH-WHO IS THAT LADY...?

...EXCUSE ME, BUT WOULD YOU LET ME GO... PLEASE?

UH...

WHY? I THOUGHT MEN WERE SUPPOSED TO LIKE... NAKED WOMEN.

BASHA
(SPLISH)

BASHA
(SPLISH)

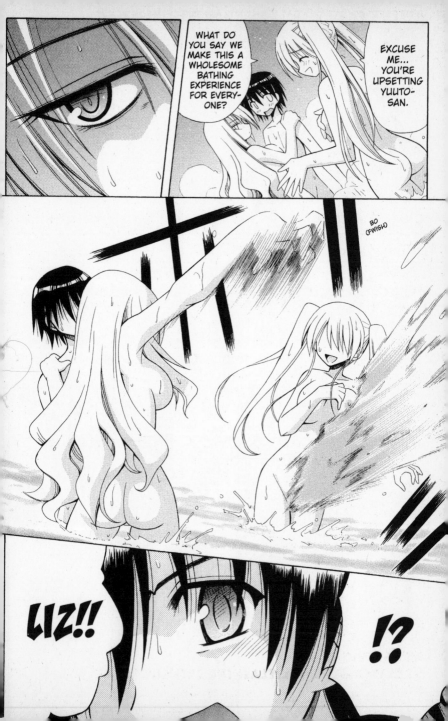

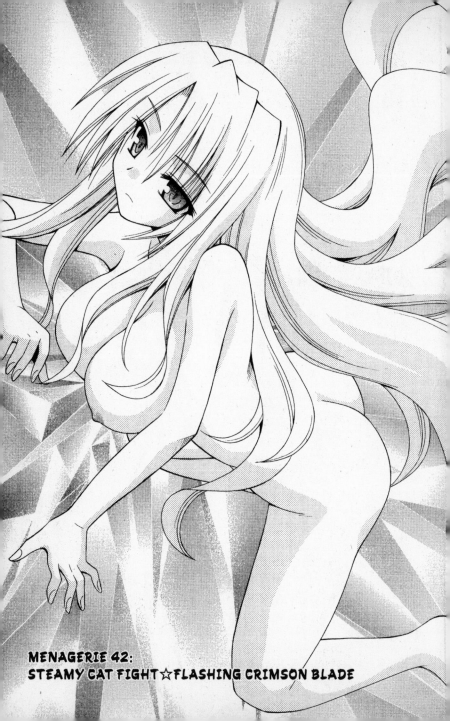

**MENAGERIE 42:
STEAMY CAT FIGHT☆FLASHING CRIMSON BLADE**

EEEK!!

BASHAA (SPLOOSH)

L I Z!!

GATATA (CLATTER)

LIZ-SAN!?

LIZ-SAN!

Y-YOU! WHY, YOU ....!!

BASHA

WHAT A LET-DOWN... YOU CAN'T FIGURE OUT MY TRUE IDENTITY WITHOUT ME UNLEASHING MY AYAKASHI AURA.

!

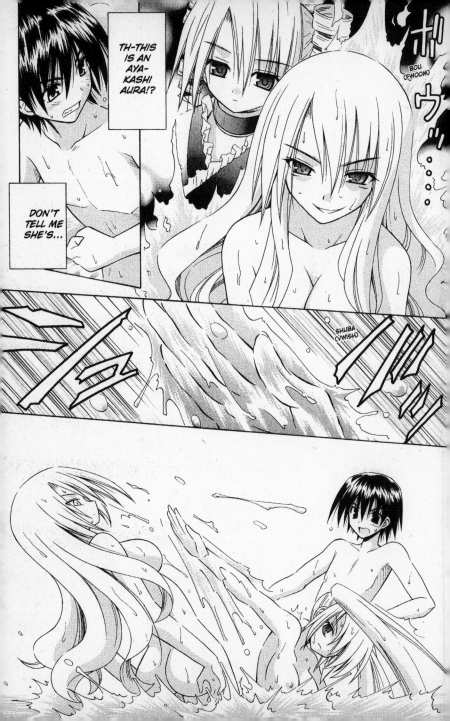

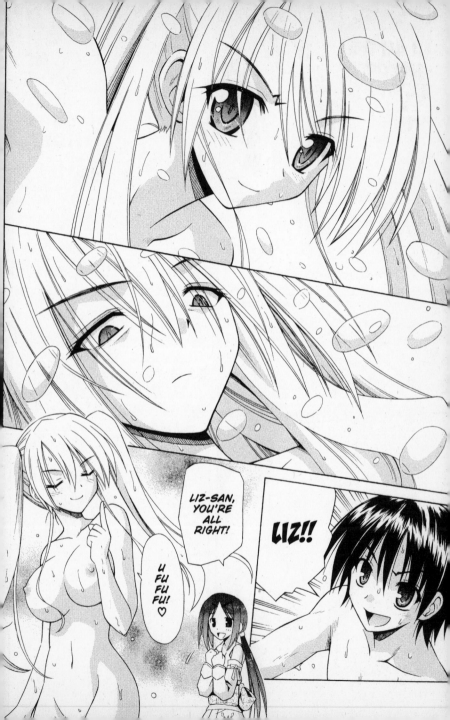

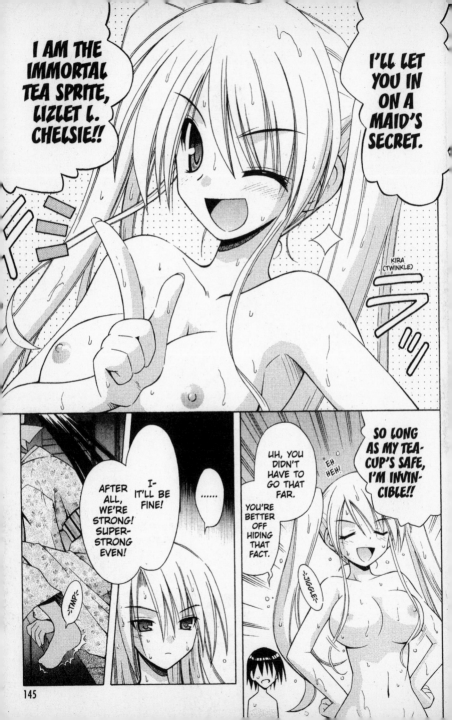

I AM THE IMMORTAL TEA SPRITE, LIZLET L. CHELSIE!!

I'LL LET YOU IN ON A MAID'S SECRET.

KIRA (TWINKLE)

AFTER ALL, WE'RE STRONG! SUPER-STRONG EVEN!

I- IT'LL BE FINE!

......

-TMP-

UH, YOU DIDN'T HAVE TO GO THAT FAR.

YOU'RE BETTER OFF HIDING THAT FACT.

EH HEH!

SO LONG AS MY TEA-CUP'S SAFE, I'M INVIN-CIBLE!!

-JIGGLE-

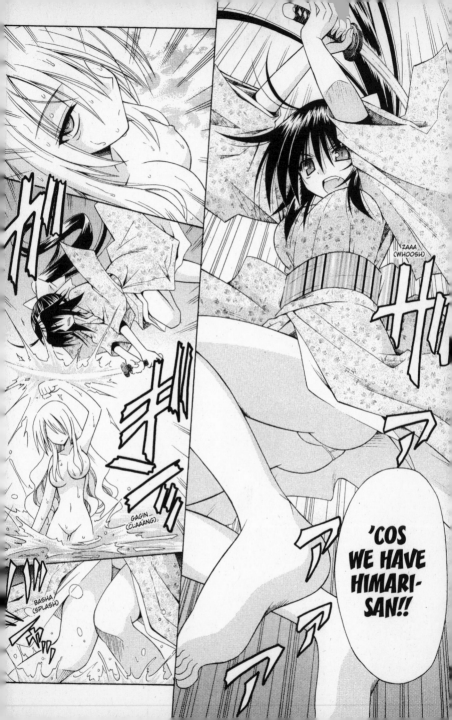

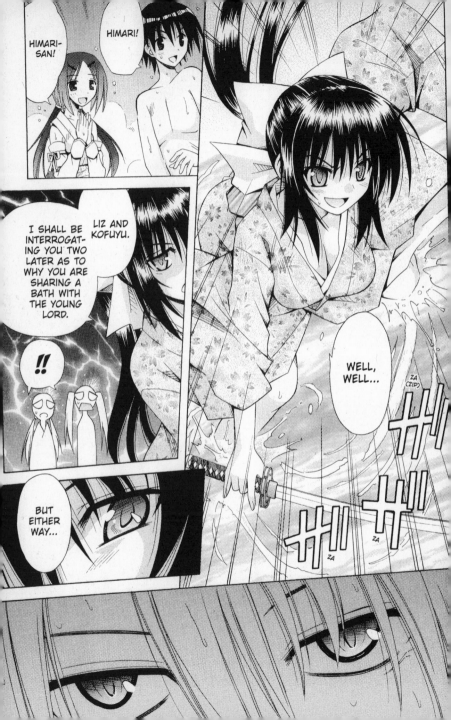

KUH
KUH
KUH
...

YOU HAVE GROWN QUITE A BIT SINCE I LAST SAW YOU.

ボイーーん
(BOIIIN (BOUNCE))

ザ (ZA (SPLASH))

SO BOTH LIZ AND THIS WENCH ARE BIGGER THAN ME...

...TCH!

EH, NINE-TAILS?

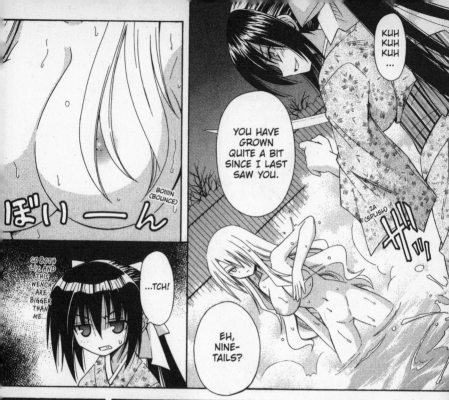

HIMARI, DON'T LET DOWN YOUR GUARD. SHUTEN-DOUJI MIGHT BE NEARBY TOO.

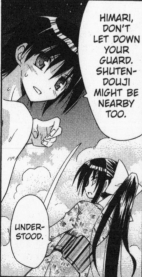

UNDER-STOOD.

TH-TH-TH-THIS LADY IS ......!?

あわ (AWA (PANIC))

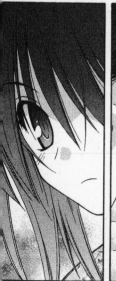

NINE-TAILS... TAMAMO-NO-MAE!?

ばしゃ (BASHA (SPLASH))

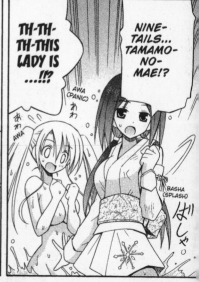

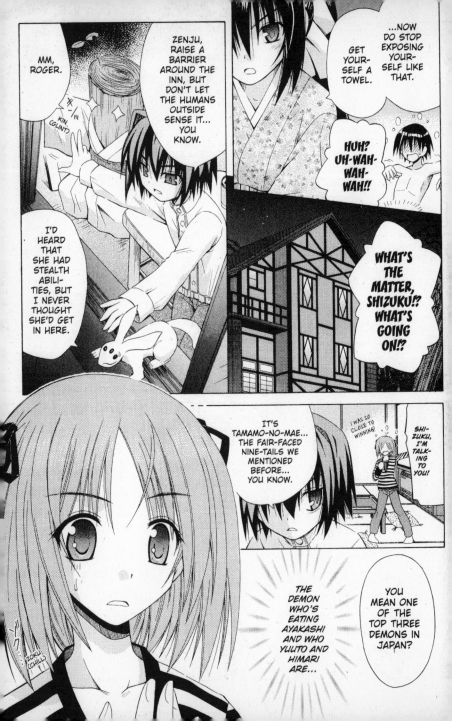

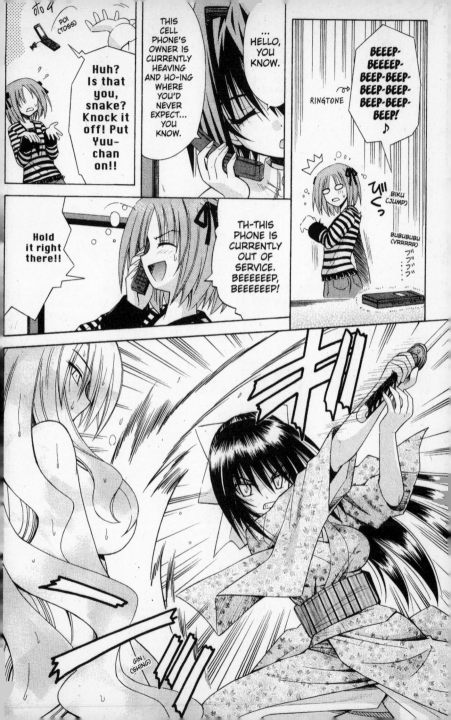

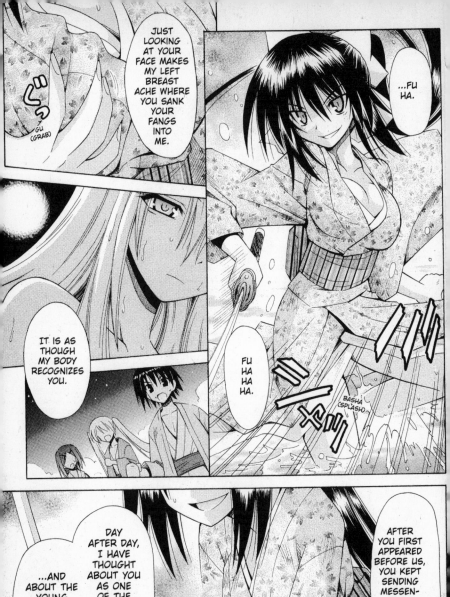

JUST LOOKING AT YOUR FACE MAKES MY LEFT BREAST ACHE WHERE YOU SANK YOUR FANGS INTO ME.

GU (GRAB)

...FU HA.

IT IS AS THOUGH MY BODY RECOGNIZES YOU.

FU HA HA HA.

BASHA (SPLASH)

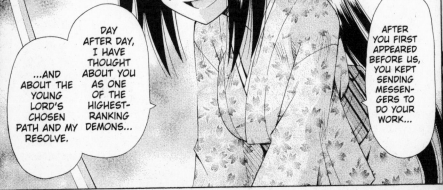

AFTER YOU FIRST APPEARED BEFORE US, YOU KEPT SENDING MESSENGERS TO DO YOUR WORK...

DAY AFTER DAY, I HAVE THOUGHT ABOUT YOU AS ONE OF THE HIGHEST-RANKING DEMONS...

...AND ABOUT THE YOUNG LORD'S CHOSEN PATH AND MY RESOLVE.

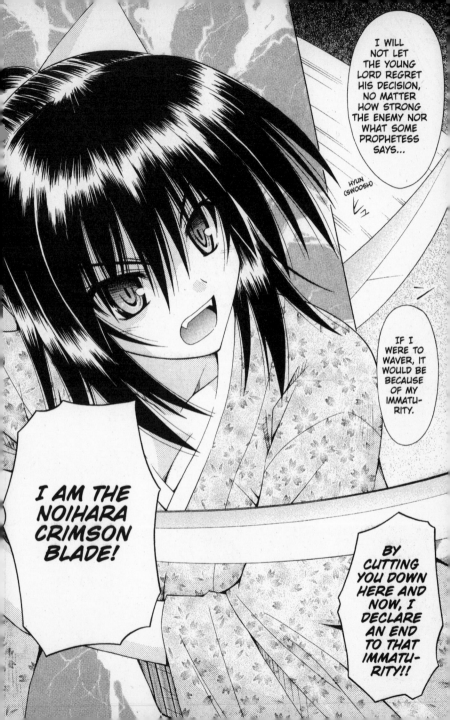

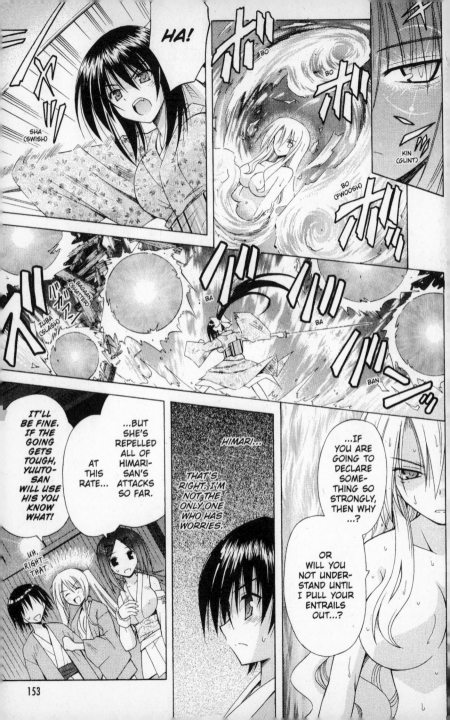

HA!

SHA
(SWISH)

BO

BO

KIN
(GLINT)

BO
(FWOOSH)

BAGAAN
(SHATTER)

ZUBA
(SLASH)

BA

BA

BAN

IT'LL BE FINE. IF THE GOING GETS TOUGH, YUUTO-SAN WILL USE HIS YOU KNOW WHAT!

...BUT SHE'S REPELLED ALL OF HIMARI-SAN'S ATTACKS SO FAR.

AT THIS RATE...

HIMARI...

THAT'S RIGHT, I'M NOT THE ONLY ONE WHO HAS WORRIES.

...IF YOU ARE GOING TO DECLARE SOMETHING SO STRONGLY, THEN WHY...?

OR WILL YOU NOT UNDERSTAND UNTIL I PULL YOUR ENTRAILS OUT...?

UH, RIGHT. THAT.

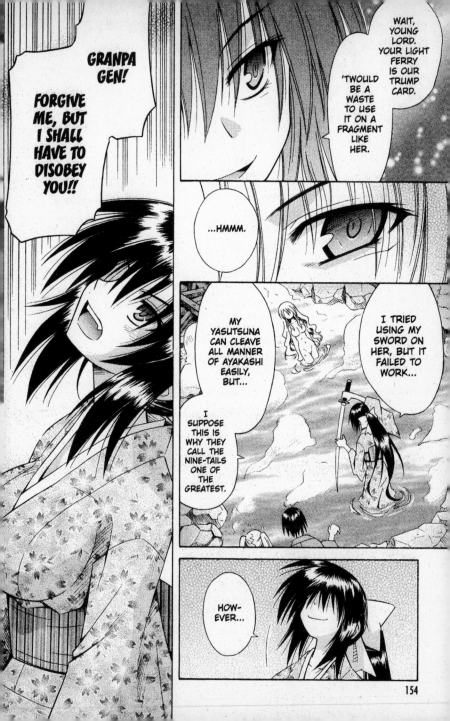

GRANPA GEN!

FORGIVE ME, BUT I SHALL HAVE TO DISOBEY YOU!!

WAIT, YOUNG LORD. YOUR LIGHT FERRY IS OUR TRUMP CARD.

'TWOULD BE A WASTE TO USE IT ON A FRAGMENT LIKE HER.

...HMMM.

MY YASUTSUNA CAN CLEAVE ALL MANNER OF AYAKASHI EASILY, BUT...

I SUPPOSE THIS IS WHY THEY CALL THE NINE-TAILS ONE OF THE GREATEST.

I TRIED USING MY SWORD ON HER, BUT IT FAILED TO WORK...

HOW-EVER...

154

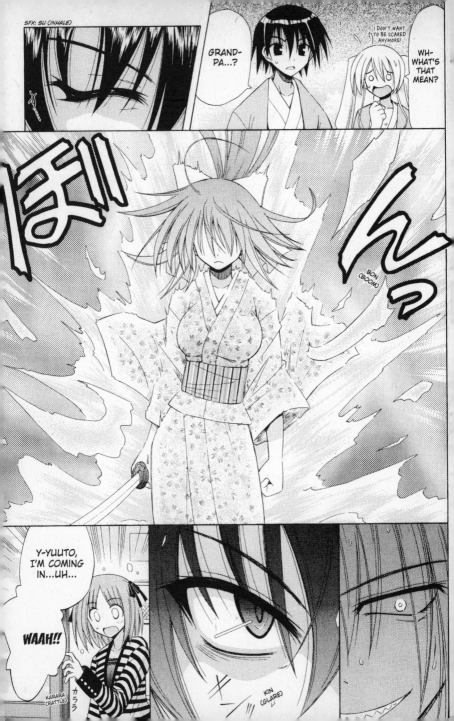

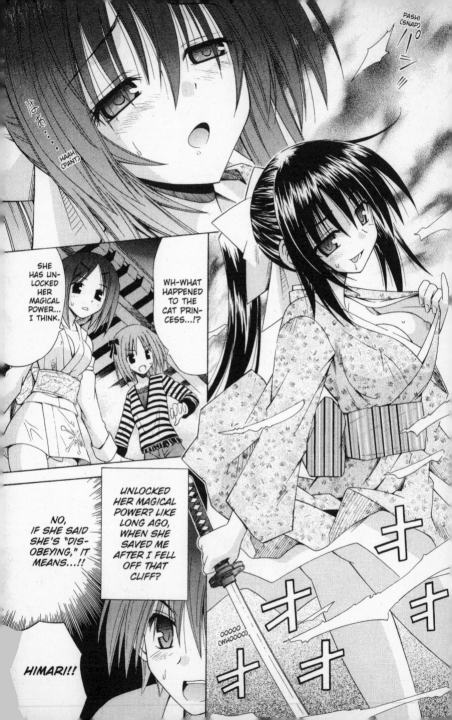

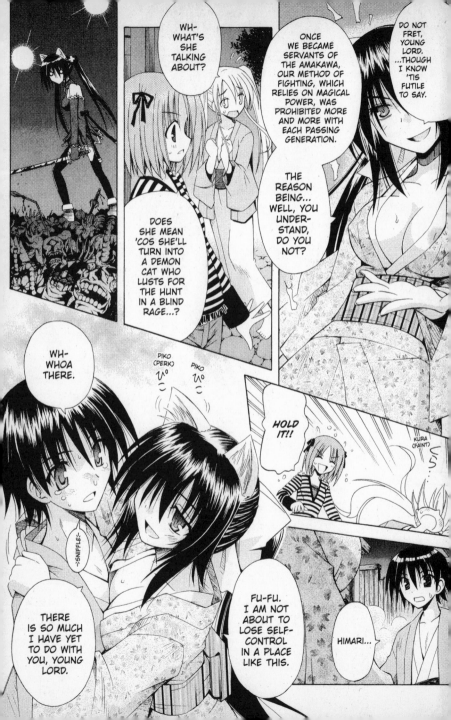

WH-WHAT'S SHE TALKING ABOUT?

ONCE WE BECAME SERVANTS OF THE AMAKAWA, OUR METHOD OF FIGHTING, WHICH RELIES ON MAGICAL POWER, WAS PROHIBITED MORE AND MORE WITH EACH PASSING GENERATION.

DO NOT FRET, YOUNG LORD. ...THOUGH I KNOW 'TIS FUTILE TO SAY.

THE REASON BEING... WELL, YOU UNDERSTAND, DO YOU NOT?

DOES SHE MEAN 'COS SHE'LL TURN INTO A DEMON CAT WHO LUSTS FOR THE HUNT IN A BLIND RAGE...?

WH-WHOA THERE.

PIKO (PERK)

PIKO

HOLD IT!!

KURA (FAINT)

~SNIFFLE~

THERE IS SO MUCH I HAVE YET TO DO WITH YOU, YOUNG LORD.

FU-FU. I AM NOT ABOUT TO LOSE SELF-CONTROL IN A PLACE LIKE THIS.

HIMARI...

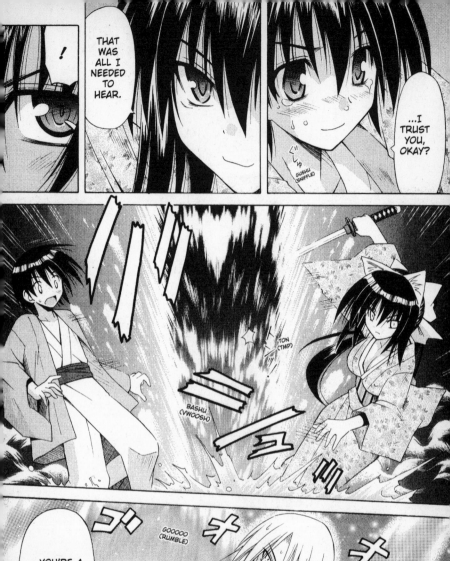

THAT WAS ALL I NEEDED TO HEAR.

!

...I TRUST YOU, OKAY?

GUSHU (SNIFFLE)

TON (TMP)

BASHU (VWOOSH)

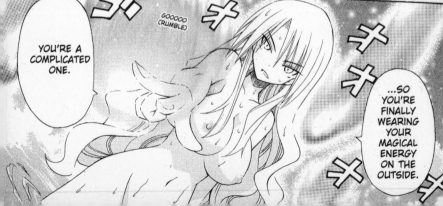

YOU'RE A COMPLICATED ONE.

GOOOOO (RUMBLE)

...SO YOU'RE FINALLY WEARING YOUR MAGICAL ENERGY ON THE OUTSIDE.

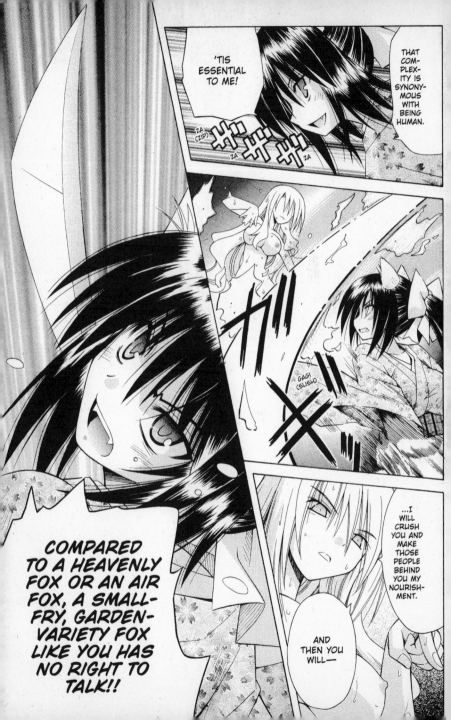

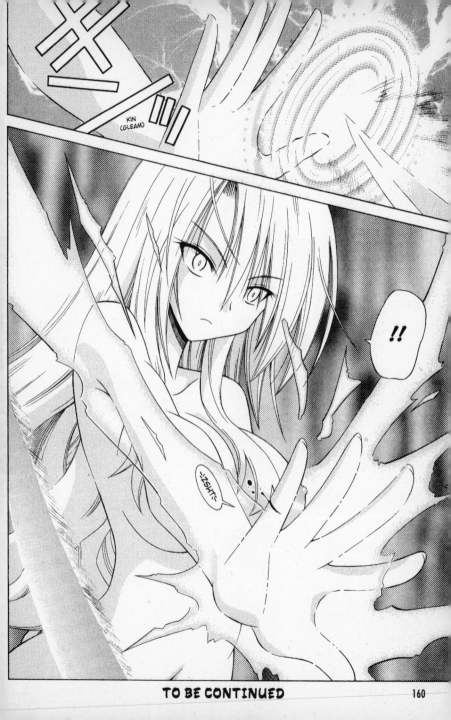

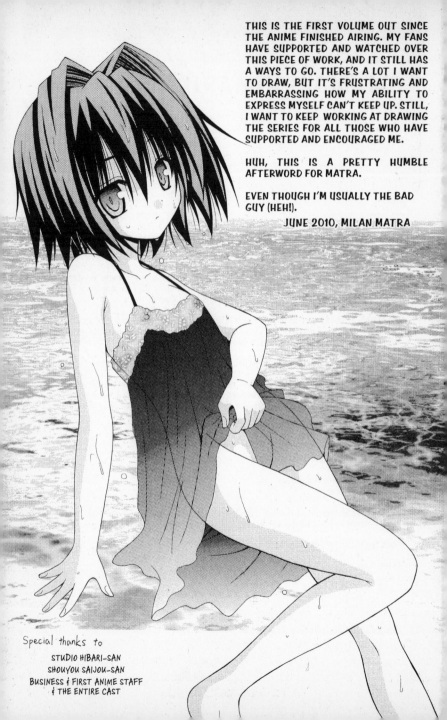

THIS IS THE FIRST VOLUME OUT SINCE THE ANIME FINISHED AIRING. MY FANS HAVE SUPPORTED AND WATCHED OVER THIS PIECE OF WORK, AND IT STILL HAS A WAYS TO GO. THERE'S A LOT I WANT TO DRAW, BUT IT'S FRUSTRATING AND EMBARRASSING HOW MY ABILITY TO EXPRESS MYSELF CAN'T KEEP UP. STILL, I WANT TO KEEP WORKING AT DRAWING THE SERIES FOR ALL THOSE WHO HAVE SUPPORTED AND ENCOURAGED ME.

HUH, THIS IS A PRETTY HUMBLE AFTERWORD FOR MATRA.

EVEN THOUGH I'M USUALLY THE BAD GUY (HEH!).

JUNE 2010, MILAN MATRA

Special thanks to

STUDIO HIBARI-SAN
SHOUYOU SAIJOU-SAN
BUSINESS & FIRST ANIME STAFF
& THE ENTIRE CAST

OMAMORI HIMARI❼

MILAN MATRA

Translation: Christine Dashiell • Lettering: Kelly Donovan

OMAMORI HIMARI Volume 7 © MATRA MILAN 2010. First published in Japan in 2010 by FUJIMISHOBO CO., LTD., Tokyo. English translation rights arranged with KADOKAWA SHOTEN Co., Ltd., Tokyo through TUTTLE-MORI AGENCY, INC., Tokyo.

Yen Press
Hachette Book Group
237 Park Avenue, New York, NY 10017

www.HachetteBookGroup.com
www.YenPress.com

Yen Press is an imprint of Hachette Book Group, Inc. The Yen Press name and logo are trademarks of Hachette Book Group, Inc.

First Yen Press Edition: May 2012

ISBN: 978-0-316-19574-4

10 9 8 7 6 5 4 3

BVG

Printed in the United States of America